EDITOR: MA

OSPREY MILITARY MEN-AT-A 36

FREDERICK S
ARMY | CAVALRY

Text by
PHILIP HAYTHORNTHWAITE
Colour plates by
BRYAN FOSTEN

Published in 1991 by
Osprey Publishing Ltd
59 Grosvenor Street, London W1X 9DA
© Copyright 1991 Osprey Publishing Ltd

British Library Cataloguing in Publication Data
Frederick the Great's army. – (Men-at-arms series,
v. 236).
   Vol. 1: Cavalry
   1. Germany. Armies, history
   I. Haythornthwaite, Philip J. (Philip John) 1951–
   357.10943

   ISBN 1–85532–134–3

Filmset in Great Britain
Printed through Bookbuilders Ltd, Hong Kong

Artist's note
Readers may care to note that the original paintings
from which the colour plates in this book were
prepared are available for private sale. All
reproduction copyright whatsoever is retained by the
publisher. All enquiries should be addressed to:
   Bryan Fosten
   5 Ross Close
   Nyetimber
   Nr. Bognor Regis
   Sussex PO21 3JW
The publishers regret that they can enter into no
correspondence upon this matter.

For a catalogue of all books published by Osprey Military
please write to:

**The Marketing Manager,
Consumer Catalogue Department,
Osprey Publishing Ltd,
Michelin House, 81 Fulham Road,
London SW3 6RB**

INTRODUCTION

The Prussian army of King Frederick II, 'the Great', became so renowned as a result of its campaigns, principally during the Seven Years' War, that it was regarded as a model for many of the other armies of Europe. Its success was founded on the fact that it was led by one of the greatest commanders of history; and its quality was refined by Frederick's methods and leadership, which transformed what was in many cases unpromising material into an army generally unsurpassed in Europe.

Frederick's infantry is most often regarded as the cornerstone of his military system, the resilience of which allowed Prussia to survive and ultimately to emerge triumphant from a war against most of the great European powers, which by all normal reckoning should have resulted in the extinction of Prussia, or at least its reduction to the insignificant state it had been before the days of Frederick William, 'the Great Elector' (reigned 1640–88). Yet the excellence of the infantry was not founded on the actions of Frederick the Great, but upon those of his father, King Frederick William I; upon his accession to the throne in 1740 Frederick II inherited an infantry force already in a state of great proficiency. It was upon the cavalry, which at times was a force equally as decisive as the infantry, that Frederick's methods had their greatest effect.

Frederick William's infantry was, in the opinion of his successor, a 'splendid instrument'; conversely, Frederick the Great found the cavalry in a desperate state. Proficient only at ceremonial drill on foot, Frederick claimed that they could not manage their horses and were commanded by officers totally ignorant of what was required of them in action. The cuirassiers he described as 'giants on elephants', who could neither manoeuvre nor fight, and who fell off their horses even on parade; they were so bad, he claimed, that 'it isn't worth the devil's while' to use them.

The reforms and training Frederick instituted had remarkably rapid effects, even though bad behaviour could still be observed as late as the Seven Years' War. (For example, with notable exceptions, cavalry performance at

'Old Fritz': King Frederick II, 'the Great', wearing the undress coat which he favoured, generally somewhat dishevelled and snuff-stained. (Engraving by Bartolozzi after Ramberg)

Kolin was so unimpressive that the hussar general Warnery remarked that issuing orders to them was akin to talking to a wall.)

Probably the most significant reason for the cavalry's rapid improvement, and its later maintenance of high standards, was the calibre of men from which it was recruited. One reason for the rigid discipline enforced in the Prussian service was to ameliorate the bane of the army, desertion: as Frederick himself admitted, 'Our regiments are composed of half our own people and half foreigners who enlist for money: the latter only wait for a favourable opportunity to quit a service to which they have no particular attachment.' (This, and succeeding quotations from Frederick, are taken from his various *Instructions* issued to his generals, which provide a unique insight into his methods. Initially secret documents, they were soon circulated and published in translations throughout Europe; the English edition of 1818 is probably the most accessible, its re-publication immediately after the military revolution occasioned by the Napoleonic Wars being testimony to the good sense represented by the *Instructions*, which were not just applicable to Frederick's own era.)

The cavalry contained the smallest proportion of desertion-prone impressed peasants and unreliable mercenaries; indeed, Frederick's *Instructions* indicate that the presence of cavalry picquets were a principal discouragement to desertion, so the cavalry had to be reliable. Most of the heavy cavalry (cuirassiers and dragoons) were drawn from the independent peasantry, many of whom had experience of working with horses from their agricultural background; and although Frederick initially recruited Hungarians and similar wild elements for his hussars, he later experienced no difficulty in finding suitable recruits for the light cavalry, from the attractions of loot and the less restrained lifestyle of hussar service.

Men and mounts

Frederick reduced the ponderous size of his 'heavies' from the 'giants on elephants' he had inherited, but the fact that the effectiveness of cuirassiers depended upon their physical presence and the impetus of a charge on large horses meant that they remained the largest men: the minimum height for cuirassiers and dragoons was 5 ft. 5 in., with horses in proportion. Conversely, the rapid movement required of hussars needed smaller men, so that their maximum height was 5 ft. 5 in. Supply of suitable horses was more difficult; the heavy regiments were mounted principally upon the powerful north German breed and the hussars upon lighter and swifter so-called 'Polish' horses, purchased in Poland, Russia and the Balkans. The darkest horses were the best in contemporary estimation, and were thus allocated to the cuirassiers. The protracted campaigning of the Seven Years' War, however, made it impossible for standards to be maintained; although the cuirassiers continued to be mounted on German horses, the lighter breeds had to be utilised for dragoons, initially for rear ranks but eventually for entire regiments.

The calibre of officer increased markedly under Frederick's insistence that his officers 'secure the friendship and confidence of the private soldier . . . if in any affair he knows how to conduct himself agreeably to the dispositions of the people under him, the execution of it will be more easy, pleasant, and certain'. The discovery of talented cavalry leaders, most famously the dissolute cuirassier general Friedrich Wilhelm von Seydlitz, and the irreplaceable hussar Hans Joachim von Zieten, was an invaluable assistance to Frederick.

Rigorous training was another factor: at least when conditions permitted, cavalrymen were given two years' schooling to turn them not only into a disciplined, cohesive body, but also into excellent horsemen, in which Seydlitz personally led the way—a magnificent rider, he was capable of lifting his hat off the ground with a sabre-point, at a gallop. Frederick regularly trained his army in peacetime not only in barrack-square manoeuvres, but in large-scale exercises which resembled real campaigns, and thus the various elements of the army were used to collaborating in combined operations. Unlike the Austrian service, in which hussars were independent of the rest and regarded as somewhat barbaric Hungarian tribesmen, in Frederick's army there was some interchange of personnel between light and heavy regiments (even Seydlitz had commanded a hussar squadron in the Second Silesian War) so that each was aware of the other's characteristics.

Tactics

Organisation for combat was determined by the capabilities of the various elements, though exigencies of service did not always allow the cavalry to be utilised in the 'ideal' manner envisaged by Frederick. (Each of the three 'arms' was supposedly capable of performing the duties of the others: Frederick's stated aim was that the cuirassiers and dragoons 'should be as adroit as the hussars', and that the hussars 'should be able to charge with as much cohesion' as the heavier regiments; this was largely achieved, except that the cuirassiers were not ideal for reconnaissance duties).

When assembled in line-of-battle, the ideal formation was for the first line to be composed of cuirassiers, with no more than ten paces between squadrons, arrayed like a wall (*en muraille*) to ride down the enemy. The second line acted as the immediate support for the first, to cover gaps and deal with any enemy who broke through; and instead of simply following the first line, were also to manoeuvre on the enemy's flanks and engage his supports. Dragoons were ideally employed in this role, having much of the impetus of a cuirassier charge but capable of more rapid

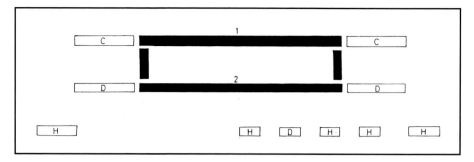

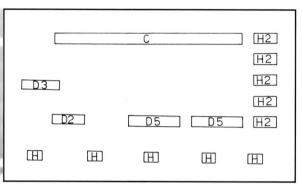

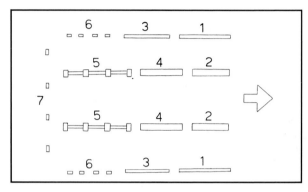

The right wing of an army, as specified in 1744; numerals indicate the number of squadrons in each body: (C) cuirassiers as first line cavalry: twenty squadrons or more. (D) dragoons: second line cavalry, 15 squadrons (three regiments). (H) hussars: ten squadrons as flank-protection, five squadrons as third line.

Advance of an army in columns, showing disposition of cavalry: (1) first line cavalry—generally cuirassiers; (2) first line infantry; (3) second line cavalry—generally dragoons; (4) second line infantry; (5) baggage-train with cavalry escorts; (6) one regiment of hussars on each flank deployed in squadrons, flank-protection for baggage; (7) one regiment of hussars, deployed in squadrons, as rear-guard.

manoeuvre. The third line acted as a general reserve for the whole army, to cover any breakthroughs and especially to pursue a beaten enemy: the speed of manoeuvre required meant that this was the best employment for hussars. It was forbidden fully to commit the third line until the battle was decided, at least four squadrons being held as a mobile reserve until the enemy infantry was actually in flight.

These regulations were not enforced slavishly, however; Frederick allowed his generals freedom of action. He put especial importance on the abilities of the commander of the second line, who if necessary was to use part of his command to extend the first line if the enemy made a flanking movement, in which case he was to take squadrons from the third line to replace those advanced from the second; and to avoid confusion, the second line had always to be at least 300 yards behind the first. The third-line commander was also to 'act for himself', without orders, to support a threatened wing or to attack in the flank an enemy pursuing a broken Prussian wing, to stall the pursuit and enable the retiring Prussians to rally. Freder-

ick noted a variation in these tactics, should the second line be composed of the heaviest cavalry whose ability for rapid manoeuvre was thus restricted: in such circumstances, although the second-line commander was still to follow the charge of the first line, his troops had to be kept compact and not disordered, and prepare to receive prisoners routed by the first line.

The principal tactical unit was the squadron, only secondly the regiment; no permanent brigade system existed. Two methods of approach to an enemy were possible: either at right-angles with the squadrons deploying progressively from line-of-march into line-of-battle, or approaching parallel to the enemy and wheeling right or left as necessary, the latter being the preferred method. For battle, squadrons were initially formed three ranks deep, though by late 1757 a two-rank line had been adopted, initially to compensate for a shortage of men, but retained when it was found to be more effective; although the three-rank line remained the official (though rarely practised) disposition. Hussars always formed in two ranks.

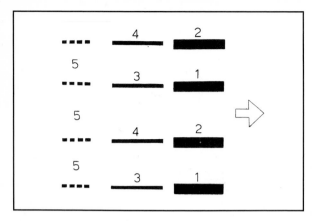

Advance of an army in 'wings', prior to engaging the enemy and thus with baggage not included: (1) first line infantry; (2) second line infantry; (3) first line cavalry—generally cuirassiers; (4) second line cavalry—generally dragoons; (5) hussars.

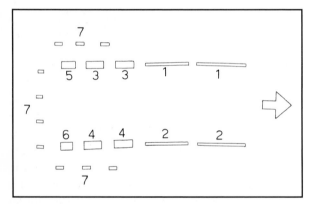

Retreat of an army in two wings, showing disposition of cavalry: (1) right wing cavalry; (2) left wing cavalry; (3) right wing infantry; (4) left wing infantry; (5) right wing rearguard: 3 battalions of infantry; (6) left wing rearguard: 3 battalions of infantry; (7) ten hussar squadrons, deployed to cover rearguard. The designation 'right' and 'left' was made with the army facing the enemy, not when facing the direction of retreat.

The charge

Great importance was placed upon the spirit and rapidity of the attack, in which no check was to be made and no firearms used, the impetus of the charge with the sabre being paramount. (Frederick William I had appreciated the merits of the charge with the sabre and had forbidden his dragoons to use firearms at this juncture: in fact, despite the deficiencies, the cavalry he inherited was probably not so inept as Frederick the Great later stated.) The object of the charge, wrote Frederick, was to 'overset the enemy by the furious shocks of our cavalry. By means of this impetuosity, the coward is hurried away, and obliged to do his duty as well as the bravest; no single trooper can be useless. The whole depends upon the *spirit* of the attack'.

The actual mechanism of the charge was specified by Frederick on a number of occasions, to be built up from the trot and delivered at the gallop; in 1742 he decreed that the gallop must commence 100 paces from the enemy, but in 1744 from 200 paces. Frederick's demands increased with the proficiency of his cavalry; in 1750 he ordered a 1,200-yard advance to be covered half at a trot and half a gallop, and in 1754 4,000 yards at a trot, 1,800 at a gallop and the last 300–400 at top speed. It remained critical that cohesion be maintained until the very moment of impact. As the charge was delivered the troops were to stand in their stirrups and raise their swords in the air (not 'point' them), to prepare for a downward cut on the enemy's head or body. (The cavalry seems generally to have ridden with 'long' stirrups: Frederick decreed that a hand's breadth between seat and saddle was sufficient when standing in the stirrups, or two hands' breadth for hussars.)

Frederick stressed that the cavalry should always charge, never *be* charged: a revealing comment is an Austrian excuse for their failure to attack at Hohenfriedberg—that there was a morass in their path, but also that the Prussians charged them first! This spirit

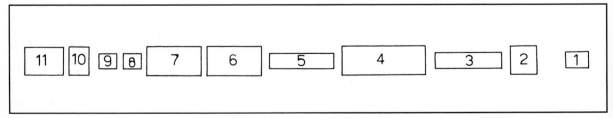

Composition of a vanguard of an army on the march, showing disposition of cavalry: (1) Dragoon detachment, one or two squadrons, leading the column and preceded by scouting parties; (2) Grenadier battalion; (3) Five squadrons of dragoons; (4) Three grenadier battalions; (5) Five squadrons of dragoons; (6) Two grenadier battalions; (7) Infantry regiment; (8) 'Grand guard' of cavalry—detachment to secure camping ground; (9) 'Small encampment'—cavalry baggage; (10) 'Grand guard' of infantry; (11) Main baggage.

Friedrich Wilhelm von Seydlitz (1721–83), Frederick's great commander of heavy cavalry. This print after Richard Knötel shows him in the uniform of his 8th Cuirassiers, with the regimental distinctions of blue facings, silver lace, blue lace on the turnbacks and red cuirass-edging. The off-white shabraque and holster caps bear the regimental black eagle device, with silver lace and fringe used by officers. Note also the gilt scales on the rear straps of the cuirass.

of offence was one of Frederick's cardinal rules for success; others included the simultaneous mass action of the whole force available, with one common aim, not charges by individual squadrons upon scattered targets; that if possible the greater weight of the charge should be delivered upon a flank; and that surprise should be achieved by advancing under cover wherever possible, as performed most spectacularly by Seydlitz at Rossbach.

Once the charge was delivered and the enemy broken, great importance was placed upon the ability to rally quickly and effectively, so as better to renew the attack or resist a counter-charge (hence the stress placed upon the maintenance of a formed reserve in the third line). The rally was to be made as quickly as possible after the enemy's flight; it was stated especially that troopers were not to look for their own place in the ranks, or even their own company, but to reform the squadron in whatever way they could to perform the process at maximum speed.

Skirmishing

Skirmishing and reconnaissance were equally vital, and although normally the preserve of hussars, 'hussar service' was taught to all. In reconnoitring, officers were exhorted not to engage the enemy but to behave with circumspection and remember that their task was to gather information: 'In war, the skin of a fox is at times as necessary as that of a lion, for cunning may succeed where force fails.'

When skirmishing, although hussars could fire their carbines from the saddle, not more than one troop of each squadron was to be deployed in open order with firearms, the remainder keeping in close order in readiness to engage with the sabre. Against Austrian light troops, Frederick ordered that his skirmishers of dragoons and hussars should always advance hastily and 'attack them closely formed and sword in hand, as this is a sort of rencontre which they cannot endure, it has always happened that we have beaten them, without paying regard to the superiority of their numbers'. If attacked by enemy skirmishers, hussars were to 'attack their adversary vigorously, though they should be fired upon, and never suffer themselves to give way, but fall resolutely on them without making any use of their firearms'.

Conversely, instead of the speed employed in the attack, Frederick instructed that when withdrawing, skirmishers should move as slowly as possible and contest every defile or bridge, 'to suffer the bad horses to gain ground, and the good ones to get wind', riders with bad horses always being directed to retire first.

Despite the emphasis placed on the sabre, dragoons were taught to fight on foot as proficiently as infantry, and even hussars could fight dismounted if necessary: on the day before Leuthen dismounted hussars stormed and captured the town of Neumarkt with as much ability in street-fighting as if they had been grenadiers. Alterna-

The charge of Seydlitz's cuirassiers at Freiberg, October 1762, illustrating the method of the charge, the troopers knee-to-knee (en muraille) with swords raised. (Engraving after Adolph Menzel)

HEAVY CAVALRY

Frederick's heavy cavalry comprised the regiments of cuirassiers and dragoons (although the latter retained aspects of the mounted-infantry service which was the origin of dragoons, they were employed in a similar manner to the cuirassiers). Frederick inherited twelve regiments of cuirassiers, each composed of five squadrons, each squadron of two companies of two platoons each. Squadron-strength was generally set at 6 officers, 12 NCOs, 4 musicians (2 trumpeters, 2 drummers), 150–160 troopers, one or two farriers and a small number of orderlies. A small regimental staff raised the regimental establishment to include 37 officers and 70 NCOs, and the total of a regiment's personnel to about 870, increasing to 890 from 1755. Not all were combatants: there was provision for about 740 troop-horses per regiment, plus a further 80 mounts for the officers.

In addition to the twelve regiments, the nucleus of a thirteenth was formed in 1740 by the creation of the Garde du Corps, ranking as the 13th Cuirassiers but initially comprising only a single squadron, intended (as the name suggests) as the royal bodyguard. Two more squadrons were added in 1756, but for active service the regiment was brigaded with the 10th Cuirassiers.

Frederick maintained twelve dragoon regiments, of which the 3rd was originally styled 'Horse Grenadiers' (*Grenadiere zu Pferde*), a designation lost in 1741 after bad conduct in action at Baumgarten (at Mollwitz, shortly after, they fled). The 4th and 9th Regts. were formed in 1741 (the former from the 3rd), the 12th was taken from Württemberg service in 1742, and the 10th formed in 1743. Establishment was generally like that of the cuirassiers, but the 5th and 6th Regts. each had ten squadrons, instead of five.

Hairstyles of the heavy cavalry included a very long queue bound with black tape, and rolls over the ears; moustaches were worn, but officers were clean-shaven. Perhaps as befitted the army of a commander notably lax about his own appearance, Frederick's army was not troubled by frequently changing sets of dress regulations. With notable exceptions like the change of colour of the dragoon uniform, Prussian cavalry uniforms remained generally constant in basic pattern throughout Frederick's reign, though as with civilian dress there was a gradual

tively, cuirassiers were trained to fight on foot only when they were surprised when dismounted, to delay the enemy sufficiently to enable them to mount and re-form.

The result of the improvements in Frederick's cavalry was to provide him with a force equally as important as his infantry. The proficiency and resulting high morale attained by the cavalry, coupled with the abilities of Frederick's cavalry commanders, enabled his mounted arm to act not merely as a support but as a decisive force in its own right, as demonstrated in such immortal victories as Rossbach and Leuthen.

(Other mounted troops, for example *Frei-Korps*, were employed by Frederick in addition to the regular regiments described here; these will be covered in Part III of this study).

Regimental titles

Regiments were customarily referred to by the name of their colonel or *Chef* (not necessarily the colonel-in-chief: the Garde du Corps, whose *Chef* was the King, could be described by the name of its commanding officer). This system can be extremely confusing: the 4th Dragoons, for example, in addition to its number, had ten different titles during Frederick's reign; whilst both the 3rd and 7th Hussars were styled 'Malachowski', albeit after different *Chefs* of that name. To assist in identification of units referred to in contemporary sources only by their name, the regimental lists which follow include the identity (with one forename) of the *Chef*, with the month of his appointment.

The rout of the Prussian right wing at Mollwitz, when the imperfections in the Prussian cavalry were redressed by the infantry; the 10th and 11th Cuirassiers were among the cavalry dispersed on the right wing. (After Menzel)

change of style over the years, the coats tending to become less voluminous and the original tricorn hat having its front 'peak' flattened, which ultimately produced the bicorn hat. (It should be noted that Adolph Menzel's illustrations, among the greatest of all uniform art, have a tendency to show semi-bicorns instead of the original tricorn, though when an early date is ascribed to Menzel's figures he does show the truly three-cornered hat of the period.) But although the uniform did not in general change radically during Frederick's reign, the army was very careful of its dress, an immaculate appearance being an element in the maintenance of discipline; and regimental distinctions were extremely varied.

CUIRASSIERS

The cuirassier uniform was similar to that worn by a number of armies, its colouring originally a copy of the leather 'buff-coat' which had been almost universal for cavalry from the early 17th century. The Prussian cuirassier coat was consequently originally straw-yellow, a shade which varied from a marked yellow colour to buff or off-white; as it was found difficult to achieve a uniform shade due to variations in the dye, eventually white coats became universal. The coat (*Kollet*) had short skirts with wide turnbacks, and facing-coloured deep gauntlet cuffs and folding collar; it had neither lapels nor buttons on the breast, but fastened to the waist with hooks and eyes, and the collar did not extend to the front of the neck. A wide strip of regimental lace edged both sides of the breast opening (not quite up to the neck), and continued around the edge of the turnbacks; similar lace edged the top and rear opening of the cuffs. The rank and file had narrow straps at the rear of the shoulder, in the colour of the body of the coat (red for the 10th, red with silver centre for the

13th), fastened with a button near the collar, to secure the straps of the cuirass.

Beneath the *Kollet* was worn a long-skirted waistcoat of the facing colour (except 10th Regt., dark blue) with an edging down the front and around the skirts of narrower lace in the regimental design. Breeches and gauntlets were white or off-white, and long white stockings or gaiters were worn under the high-topped black leather riding boots, which had spurs attached by 'leathers'. All except officers and musicians wore a wide girdle of the facing colour around the waist, under the cuirass; the stock was of stiff, black fabric.

The tricorn hat had iron reinforcing-bars or a 'secrete' internally, coloured cords around the base of the crown and rosettes in the side corners, and at the left front a black fabric cockade secured by a black loop, with a button at the lower end. From 1762 white feather plumes were adopted, to aid in distinguishing between Prussian and Austrian cuirassiers, who wore a similar uniform; the plumes had a black tip for NCOs and a black base for officers.

The cuirass consisted of a front-plate only, secured by leather straps which ran along the front of the waist of the cuirass and crossed over the wearer's back; originally of buff-yellow leather, they were whitened after the Seven Years' War. Cuirasses were enamelled black (polished for the 13th), with edges in the facing-colour.

The sabre was suspended from a waistbelt of red-brown leather, worn beneath the girdle, from a frog or slings. Suspended from the same belt was the sabretache, which had a curved lower edge, the front in the regimental facing colour and bearing a conjoined 'FR' cypher below a crown, with regimental lace on all but the upper edge; it was not worn by officers or trumpeters. The sabre or *Pallasch* of 1732 pattern had a broad, straight, double-edged blade and

Cuirassiers in action. Note the gilded scales on the rear cuirass straps of the officer falling wounded, centre; and the difference in horse furniture between the officer and the troopers (left), the former carrying no valise at the rear of the saddle. (After Menzel)

a brass, semi-basket hilt with large spherical pommel and ribbed, leather-covered grip. The solid part of the 'basket' bore an embossed eagle holding a sceptre, below a large crown, with the 'FR' cypher upon the eagle's breast. The wooden scabbard was covered with dark brown or blackened leather, originally with brass mounts, changed to iron during the Seven Years' War. The sword knot had a red-brown leather strap and white fringe, the upper sections of the tassel coloured white and/or yellow, black, green, blue or red, so that each company could be distinguished by the arrangement of colours.

Over the right shoulder (left for NCOs), and atop the cuirass, was a whitened buff-leather belt (edged with regimental lace for the 10th and 13th), supporting a black leather cartridge-box (10th and 13th white), which bore an oval brass plate (white metal for the 13th) bearing the regimental insignia. Over the left shoulder, atop the cartridge-box belt, was a very wide, buff-leather belt (later whitened) edged with regimental lace, with an iron spring clip to support the carbine at the right side; it was not worn by officers, NCOs or trumpeters, none of whom carried the carbine.

Horse-furniture included a shabraque with rounded rear corners, in the regimental facing colour (save 4th and 8th, white; 10th, dark blue), edged with regimental lace and bearing a device in the rear corners, with a matching holster-cap on each side of the saddle pommel; all ranks were equipped with two pistols. At the rear of the saddle was carried a valise, atop which was carried a folded grey greatcoat, which for the rank and file was changed after 1756 for a dark blue cloak. The carbine was carried at the right of the saddle, the muzzle in a bucket attached to the lower front of the saddle, and the butt held by a leather strap at the upper right.

Non-commissioned officers wore the same uniform with rank distinctions which included the absence of a carbine and belt, black and white rosettes on the hat, black and white tassel on the sword-knot, metallic lace edging to the cuffs of the *Kollet* (design of which varied between regiments), and after 1762 the plume already specified.

Officers' uniforms were in finer materials, generally with velvet facings, with all lace (including cockade-loop) in the regimental button-colour, though Menzel shows turn-backs edged with the facing colour instead of with metallic lace. Cuirasses were enamelled black, with a gilded border set with gilt studs, and on the breast was borne a gilt escutcheon bearing a crowned royal cypher (some sources show an eagle). The shoulder straps, including those crossing on the wearer's back, were covered with gilt scales; for the 13th, cuirass and shoulder straps were white-metal. Officers' cuirasses were edged in facing-coloured, scalloped or ruched velvet.

Hat rosettes were silver with black centre; instead of the girdle, officers wore the national silver waist-sash with interwoven black lines and fringed, hanging ends. Sword knots were silver and black; no sabretaches were carried. Two designs of shabraque existed, an *Interim* pattern for ordinary wear, which was like that of the other ranks but with metallic lace decoration and fringe, and a rectangular parade shabraque with double metallic lace edging and metallic embroidery, usually including an eagle device in the rear corners.

In addition, officers also possessed a long-skirted frock coat (*Galarock*) for 'dress' occasions, which could be worn over the cuirass but was more usually worn with a long, straw-coloured waistcoat. The *Galarock* was white with cuffs, lapels and folding collar in the facing colour, and with metallic embroidery loops in a rococo, foliate design (which varied with the regiment)—three pairs of loops on each lapel, two loops on each cuff and below each lapel, two on the pocket-flap and two on the rear skirt at waist level. On the right shoulder was worn a metallic cord aiguillette. (Red coat with blue facings and no lapels for the 10th and 13th). The tricorn worn with the *Galarock* had an edging of scalloped metallic lace.

Trumpeters wore no cuirass, and a *Kollet* ornamented with the regimental pattern of musicians' lace: a wide lace on the breast, turnbacks and cuffs, and a narrow variety edging the collar, the front and rear sleeve-seams, in seven horizontal bars on each sleeve (not shown by some sources); and edging around, and as vertical bars upon, 'swallows'-nest' wings. At the rear of the *Kollet* were two cloth loops hanging from the shoulder, of the coat body-colour and edged with musicians' narrow lace, a relic of the hanging sleeves worn by trumpeters in the previous century. The waistcoat was like that of the rank and file, with ordinary, not musicians', lace; the girdle was not worn, the waistbelt (worn atop the *Kollet*) being whitened buff-leather with musicians' lace edging. Sword knots were like those of NCOs; hats were similarly of NCO pattern, plus a feather edge of the facing colour (save 3rd, 4th and 8th, red), and after 1762 a plume with facing-coloured tip.

Regimental details

In the lists which follow, only the regimental *Chefs* (and thus regimental titles) of the reign of Frederick the Great are given. There is insufficient space for details of the whole of a unit's service, but major actions are given with the following numbers: (*1*) Mollwitz, 10 April 1741; (*2*) Chotusitz, 17 May 1742; (*3*) Hohenfriedberg, 4 June 1745; (*4*) Soor, 30 September 1745; (*5*) Kesselsdorf, 15 December 1745; (*6*) Lobositz, 10 October 1756; (*7*) Prague, 6 May 1757; (*8*) Kolin, 18 June 1757; (*9*) Gross-Jägersdorf, 30 August 1757; (*10*) Breslau, 22 November 1757; (*11*) Rossbach, 5 November 1757; (*12*) Leuthen, 5 December 1757; (*13*) Krefeld, 23 June 1758; (*14*) Zorndorf, 25 August 1758; (*15*) Hochkirch, 14 October 1758; (*16*) Kay, 23 July 1759; (*17*) Minden, 1 August 1759; (*18*) Kunersdorf, 12 August 1759; (*19*) Maxen, 20 November 1759; (*20*) Liegnitz, 15 August 1760; (*21*) Torgau, 3 November 1760; (*22*) Freiberg, 29 October 1762.

1st Cuirassiers

Raised 1666. *Chefs*: July 1724 Wilhelm von Buddenbrock; April 1757 Hans von Krockow; Feb. 1759 Gustav von Schlabrendorff; Dec. 1768 Friedrich von Röder; March 1781 Gideon von Apenburg; June 1784 Philipp von Bohlen.

Actions: 2, 3, 4, 5, 7, 8, 10, 12, 15, 16, 18, 21, 22.

Uniform: red facings, white buttons. *Other ranks*: green hat-rosettes (colour of the house of Anhalt, commemorating the regiment's first colonel); red lace with two white stripes and narrow white edge. Sabretache red, all decoration in regimental lace: crowned 'FR', border of chain pattern with stripe of lace on either side. Shabraque: red, bearing crowned 'FR' in rear corners and on holster caps, edges bearing wide border within narrow border, all in regimental lace. Cartridge box plate: crowned eagle on crossed cannon-barrels. *NCOs*: double silver zigzag lace on cuff. *Officers*: silver lace; silver loops on *Galarock* shaped as a loop with tassel end. *Musicians*: red hat-feathers; narrow lace, alternate red and yellow oblongs each bearing two blue diamonds; wide lace, silver bar between two rows of narrow lace (lace designed from the colours of von Buddenbrock's coat of arms, plus regimental facing colour).

Seydlitz's cuirassiers (8th, 10th and 13th) charge broken Russian formations at Zorndorf; in such circumstances the impetus of a charge of large, armoured troopers on heavy horses was crucial. (After Menzel)

2nd Cuirassiers

Raised 1666. *Chefs*: Aug. 1730 Prince August Wilhelm of Prussia; Dec. 1758 Prince Friedrich Heinrich of Prussia (regiment known as 'Prinz Wilhelm', later 'Prinz von Preussen'); Sept. 1768 Georg von Wiersbitzky; March 1778 Christian von Weyher; Sept. 1782 Friedrich von Saher; March 1783 Karl von Backhoff.

Actions: 2, 3, 4, 6, 8, 10, 14, 18, 20, 21.

Uniform: alone of the cuirassiers, it retained coats of a very strong yellow colour, hence the name *Gelbe Reiter* ('Yellow Horse'). Dark red facings, white buttons (yellow pre-1742). *Other ranks*: white hat-rosettes, dark red lace on coat, white on waistcoat; dark red sabretache bearing white crowned 'FR', wide white lace border within narrow laces. Cartridge box plate: crowned 'FR' within ornamental border. Shabraque: dark red, white crowned 'FR', border of wide white lace within narrower lace. *NCOs*: silver lace on cuffs. *Officers*: silver lace; silver loops of rococo foliate design on *Galarock*. *Musicians*: dark red hat-feathers, silver lace with undulating dark red stripe.

3rd Cuirassiers (Leibregiment zu Pferde)

Raised 1672. *Chefs*: Nov. 1736 Adam von Wreech; Sept. 1746 Andreas von Katzler; Sept. 1747 Johann von Katte; Jan. 1758 Robert Scipio, Freiherr von Lentulus; Dec. 1778 Johann von Merian; Sept. 1782 Ernst von Kospoth.

Actions: 5, 6, 7, 8, 11, 12, 18, 20, 21, 22.

Uniform: dark blue facings, yellow buttons. *Other ranks*: red hat-rosettes, dark blue lace with white stripe; dark blue sabretache bearing crowned 'FR', edging of wide lace band between narrow bands, all in white lace with blue stripe near each edge. Cartridge-box plate: crowned 'FR' within ornamental border. Dark blue shabraque with crowned 'FR' and double lace edging, in lace as on sabretache. *NCOs*: pointed gold lace darts set at right angles to upper edge of cuff. *Officers*: gold lace, *Galarock* loops with simulated tassel ends. *Musicians*: red hat-feathers, lace gold with two dark blue stripes.

4th Cuirassiers

Raised 1674. *Chefs*: May 1733 Friedrich, Graf von Gessler; Jan. 1758 Johann von Schmettau; Sept. 1764 Hans von Woldeck-Arneburg; June 1769 Georg von Arnim; Sept. 1785 Baron Karl von Mengden.

Actions: 2, 3, 4, 7, 10, 12, 15, 21, 22.

Uniform: black facings, yellow buttons. *Other ranks*: yellow hat-rosettes, lace white with three light blue broken lines; sabretache black, bearing crowned 'FR', edging of two lines of lace with undulating line between, all in regimental lace. Cartridge-box plate edged with wreath, crowned eagle in centre. White shabraque, yellow crown over orange-yellow shield bearing black eagle in rear corners and on holster-caps, edged with wide border of regimental lace with inner border of undulating loop and chain pattern. *NCOs*: double gold lace edging to cuffs. *Officers*: gold lace, *Galarock* with foliate loops. *Musicians*: red hat-

A disconsolate Frederick is given a drink of water by an old trooper in the aftermath of Kolin: 'Drink, your majesty, and let battles be battles; it's well that you are safe. Let us trust in God that it will soon be our turn to conquer!' In this print after Richard Knötel the wounded trooper is shown wearing the uniform of the 11th Cuirassiers: light blue facings and sabretache (with white lace), and white hat-rosettes.

feathers, lace (wide) silver with two crimson stripes; narrow, silver with one crimson stripe (colours of coat of arms of Peter von Blanckensee, colonel 1714–32).

5th Cuirassiers

Raised 1683. *Chefs*: March 1712 Friedrich Wilhelm, Margrave of Brandenburg-Schwedt; May 1771 Friedrich von Lölhöffel; Feb. 1780 Maximilian von Mauschwitz; March 1782 Prince Ludwig Alexander of Württemberg.

Actions: 1, 3, 5, 7, 10, 12, 14, 16, 18, 20, 21.

Uniform: light blue facings, yellow buttons. *Other ranks*: orange hat-rosettes, lace light blue and white squares edged with alternate light blue and white oblongs; narrow lace (on waistcoat) of light blue and white oblongs with alternate light blue and white oblong edges. Light blue sabretache bearing crowned 'FR', edging of double lace with undulating line between, all in regimental 'narrow' lace design. Cartridge-box plate bore crowned 'FR'. Light blue shabraque bearing yellow crown over yellow-edged white shield bearing yellow-crowned black eagle, wide outer and undulating narrow inner border of regimental lace. *NCOs*: double gold lace on cuffs. *Officers*: gold lace, *Galarock* with foliate loops. *Musicians*: light blue hat-feathers, lace gold with light blue stripe bearing yellow diamonds. Upon the general introduction of blue cloaks in 1756, the 5th retained the previous white greatcoat for some time.

6th Cuirassiers

Raised 1688. *Chefs*: Dec. 1737 Prince Eugen of Anhalt-Dessau; March 1744 Ludwig von Stille; April 1753 Baron Georg von Schönaich; April 1759 Heinrich von Vasold; June 1769 Gustav von Seelhorst; Jan. 1779 Theophilus, Freiherr von Hoverbeck; Jan. 1781 Hans von Rohr.

Actions: 3, 5, 6, 8, 10, 12, 19.

Uniform: brick red facings, yellow buttons. *Other ranks*: brick red hat-rosettes, lace white bearing brick red stylized double star devices, edging of brick red and white oblong; brick red sabretache bearing crowned 'FR', wide lace within narrow laces border, all in regimental lace. Cartridge-box plate bore trophy of arms over crowned 'FR'. Brick red shabraque bearing yellow crown over 'FR' in narrow regimental lace in rear corners and on holster caps; double band of wide regimental lace edging. *NCOs*: gold pointed lace darts set at right angles to upper edge of cuff. *Officers*: gold lace, *Galarock* with gold foliate loops. *Musicians*: brick red hat-feathers, gold lace with alternate red and white squares on both edges.

Seydlitz's vital first charge at Rossbach, which overthrew the vanguard of the combined army. (After Menzel)

7th Cuirassiers

Raised 1688. *Chefs*: July 1733 Friedrich von Bredow; July 1755 Georg von Driesen; Nov. 1758 Christian von Horn; March 1762 Leopold von Manstein; Aug. 1777 Gustav von der Marwitz; June 1784 Friedrich von Kalckreuth.

Actions: 2, 3, 5, 6, 7, 8, 11, 12, 18, 19.

Uniform: yellow facings, white buttons. *Other ranks*: yellow hat-rosettes, yellow lace with two white stripes; yellow sabretache bearing crowned 'FR', double lace border with undulating lace between, all in regimental lace. Cartridge-box plate bore crowned 'FR'. Yellow shabraque bearing crowned 'FR', border of wide lace within narrow lace, all of regimental pattern. *NCOs*: double silver lace edge to cuffs (Menzel shows two pointed-ended silver loops). *Officers*: silver lace, *Galarock* with S-shaped foliate loops. *Musicians*: yellow hat-feathers, lace yellow with two silver stripes.

8th Cuirassiers

Raised 1691. *Chefs*: Oct. 1734 Friedrich von Waldow; May 1742 Friedrich von Rochow; Nov. 1757 Friedrich Wilhelm von Seydlitz; June 1774 Maximilian von Pannwitz.

Actions: 2, 3, 4, 5, 6, 8, 11, 12, 14, 15, 20, 21.

Uniform: See Plate A1. Dark blue facings, white buttons. *Other ranks*: red and white hat-rosettes, white lace with two blue stripes; blue sabretache bearing crowned 'FR', double lace border with chain-pattern lace between, all in regimental lace. Cartridge-box plate bore crowned eagle. White shabraque bearing yellow-crowned black eagle in rear corners and on holster caps, border of wide orange lace

Seydlitz at Rossbach.
Illustrated here are the
long stirrups favoured by
the Prussian cavalry, so
that the action of standing
in the stirrups raised the
body only a short distance
from its normal position.
(After Menzel)

Cuirassier officer:
apparently a facsimile
copy of an illustration by
C.C. Horvath, 1789.
Although this slightly
post-dates the
Frederickian period, it is
useful in illustrating
details of the Kollet, in
Frederick's time concealed
by the cuirass.

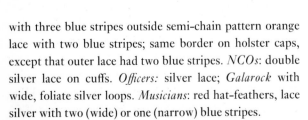

with three blue stripes outside semi-chain pattern orange
lace with two blue stripes; same border on holster caps,
except that outer lace had two blue stripes. *NCOs*: double
silver lace on cuffs. *Officers:* silver lace; *Galarock* with
wide, foliate silver loops. *Musicians:* red hat-feathers, lace
silver with two (wide) or one (narrow) blue stripes.

9th Cuirassiers

Raised 1691. *Chefs*: April 1706 Hans von Katte; June 1741
Hermann, Graf von Wartensleben; Nov. 1741 Adolf von
Möllendorff; Nov. 1743 Bernhard von Bornstedt; Sept.
1751 Prince Johann von Schönaich-Karolath (regiment
known as 'Prinz Schönaich'); Jan. 1758 Jakob von Bredow;
June 1769 Friedrich von Podewils; Sept. 1784 Christian
von Braunschweig.

Actions: 2, 3, 4, 7, 10, 12, 15, 19.

Uniform: crimson facings, yellow buttons. *Other ranks*:
crimson hat-rosettes, white lace with three crimson stripes;
crimson sabretache bearing crowned 'FR', bordered by
two narrow laces with undulating line between, all lace of
regimental pattern. Cartridge-box plate bore crowned
'FR' within wreath. Crimson shabraque, bearing orange
crown over white shield bearing yellow-crowned black
eagle, border of double regimental lace with inner border
of undulating, semi-chain pattern white lace with two
crimson stripes. *NCOs*: double gold zigzag lace on cuff.
Officers: gold lace, *Galarock* with gold foliate loops.
Musicians: crimson hat-feathers, gold lace with crimson
stripe.

10th Cuirassiers (Regiment Gens d'armes)

Raised 1691. *Chefs*: May 1739 Wolf von Pannewitz; April
1743 Georg, Freiherr von der Golz; Sept. 1747 Nikolaus
von Katzler; April 1761 Friedrich, Graf von Schwerin;
June 1768 Hans von Krusemarck; June 1775 Joachim von
Prittwitz.

Actions: 1, 3, 4, 6, 11, 12, 14, 15, 20, 21.

Uniform: red facings, yellow buttons. *Other ranks*: white
hat-rosettes, red velvet lace with gold stripe; red sabretache bearing gold crowned 'FR', wide red lace border
with gold stripe. White cartridge-box and belt, both edged
with regimental lace; plate bore crowned 'FR'. Dark blue
shabraque, rear corners and holster caps bearing gold
crown over silver star of the Order of the Black Eagle (with
orange central disc bearing eagle, green wreath at base of
disc); red lace border with three gold stripes. *NCOs*:
double gold lace edging to cuffs. *Officers*: gold lace; red
Galarock with dark blue collar and cuffs, no lapels, gold
foliate loops (on breast, spaced one over two over three). A
plainer red frock coat (*Interimsrock*) was similar, but
without lace. *Musicians*: see Plate B3.

11th Cuirassiers (Leib-Carabinier Regt.)

Raised 1691. *Chefs*: April 1738 Harmann, Graf von
Wartensleben; June 1741 Kaspar von Bredow; November

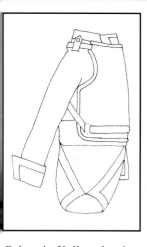

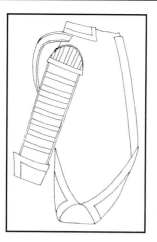

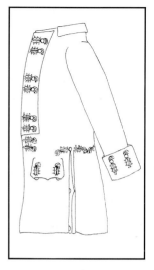

Cuirassier Kollet, *showing position of cuirass and girdle. The shoulder strap of the* Kollet *was often set to the rear of the shoulder.*

Cuirassier trumpeter's Kollet, *showing the position of the lace and imitation hanging sleeves at the rear.*

Cuirassier officer's **Galarock***; position of the embroidered loops was the same for most regiments, though the exact design of embroidery varied between units; this shows the loops with simulated tassel ends of the 2nd Regiment.*

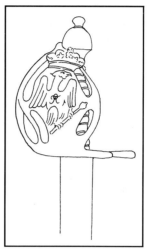

1732-pattern cuirassier sabre; brass semi-basket hilt bearing an embossed, crowned eagle design.

1751 Peter de (or 'von') Pennevaire; Jan. 1759 Joachim von Bandemer; Sept. 1768 Reinhold, Baron von Hoverbeck; Dec. 1770 Reimar von Kleist; June 1775 Philipp von Bohlen; June 1784 Heinrich von Reppert.
Actions: 1, 3, 5, 6, 7, 8, 10, 12, 14, 15, 20, 21.
Uniform: light blue facings, white buttons. *Other ranks:* white hat-rosettes, white lace with light blue stripe near each edge, and light blue diamonds with white centres down the middle. Light blue sabretache bearing crowned 'FR', double lace border with undulating lace between, all in regimental lace. Cartridge-box badge bore crowned eagle. Light blue shabraque bearing crowned 'FR', double border of regimental lace. *NCOs:* pointed silver darts at right angles to upper edge of cuff. *Officers:* silver lace, *Galarock* with silver loops with simulated tassel end. *Musicians:* light blue hat-feathers, lace as other ranks but silver instead of white.

12th Cuirassiers

Raised 1704. *Chefs:* Feb. 1728 Arnold von Waldow; April 1743 Friedrich, Freiherr, von Kyau; April 1759 Johann von Spaen; Feb. 1763 Georg von Dallwig.
Actions: 2, 3, 4, 5, 7, 8, 12, 15, 16, 18, 21.
Uniform: orange facings, yellow buttons. *Other ranks:* green hat-rosettes (the colour of Anhalt, commemorating the colonelcy of Wilhelm Gustav, Erbprinz of Anhalt-Dessau, 1715), orange lace with white stripe; orange sabretache bearing crowned 'FR', double lace border with chain-pattern lace between, all in regimental lace.

Cartridge-box badge bore scroll inscribed 'Pro Gloria et Patria' over crowned eagle, loop design around edge. Orange shabraque bearing white crown over white ovoid bearing yellow-crowned black eagle under 'Pro Gloria et Patria' scroll; white lace border with four orange stripes, inner white border of white chain-pattern lace with two orange stripes. *NCOs:* gold lace edging to cuffs. *Officers:* gold lace, *Galarock* with foliate loops. *Musicians:* orange hat-feathers, orange lace with gold stripe.

13th Cuirassiers (Garde du Corps)

Raised 1740. *Chef:* the King. Commanding officers: June 1740 Otto von Blumenthal; May 1744 Georg von Jaschin-sky; May 1747 Johann von Blumenthal; Jan. 1758 Wilhelm von Wackenitz; May 1760 Karl von Schätzell; Dec. 1773 Carl, Freiherr von Mengden; Sept. 1785 Carl von Byern.
Actions: 3, 4, 6, 7, 8, 11, 12, 14, 15, 20, 21.
Uniform: see Plates A3, B1, B2. Red facings, white buttons. *Other ranks:* white hat-rosettes, lace red velvet with silver stripe (on waistcoat, dark blue with silver edges); shoulder straps of regimental lace; red sabretache bearing silver crowned 'FR', narrow within wide silver lace border. White cartridge-box and belt, edged with regimental lace; cartridge-box plate white metal, bearing crowned 'FR'.

Red shabraque with pointed rear corners, plain but for silver lace border. White metal cuirass, white metal sabre hilt and scabbard fittings. *NCOs*: double silver lace edging to cuffs. *Officers*: silver lace, silvered cuirass; for *Galarock*, see Plate A3. *Musicians*: red hat-feathers, silver lace with one or two red stripes (narrow and wide lace respectively).

DRAGOONS

Although the dragoons had relinquished their original mounted infantry role before Frederick the Great ascended the throne, elements of their equipment indicated their infantry origin. The coat was of infantry style, with long tails, with open lapels (for most regiments), cuffs, collar and turnbacks in the facing colour; buttons were in pairs, six on each lapel, two below the right lapel with corresponding button-holes beneath the left, two on the pocket flaps and cuffs, and three on the side vent of the skirt. Coats were originally white or off-white, but from mid-1745 to early 1746 they changed to light blue; the 12th Dragoons, taken from Württemberg service in 1742, retained their light blue Württemberg coats, which may have served as the inspiration for the change in uniform-colour three years later. All ranks wore an aiguillette of the button colour from the rear of the right shoulder, and the rank and file had a shoulder strap on the left shoulder, to secure the carbine belt.

Waistcoats were single-breasted, of yellow or straw-yellow/buff, without lace; hats and legwear were like those

of the cuirassiers. Black leather cartridge boxes were carried by the rank and file from a wide buff-leather belt (whitened after the Seven Years' War) over the left shoulder, which belt also supported the carbine, which was of an intermediate length between the infantry musket and the shorter cuirassier carbine, and was equipped with a bayonet and dark red leather sling. The 1735-pattern dragoon *Pallasch* had a double-edged blade and a brass half-basket guard formed of four bars, two intersecting with a brass disc where they joined, with a short quillon at the rear and a half-shell on the opposite side of the 'basket', an eagle-head pommel and a leather grip bound with brass wire. The scabbard was covered with dark brown leather, with a brass chape and hook which fitted into a frog on the waist belt; no sabretache was carried.

Except for the 9th, NCO rank distinction was a metallic lace edging of the button colour upon the cuffs; lace was worn by the rank and file only in the 9th. Officers' coats for most regiments had metallic embroidered loops on the button-holes, and at the rear waist; their sashes were worn over the waistcoat but beneath the coat. A number of contemporary portraits show senior officers, especially in the earlier period, wearing a cuirass underneath the coat.

Musicians wore distinctive lace to edge the collar, lapels, pockets and cuffs, sometimes on the turnbacks; and on the rear and side vents of the skirts, the upper button of the side vent being set upon a rosette of lace; but on the sleeves, lace was restricted to the bottom edge of the 'swallows'-

The Bayreuth Dragoons (5th Regt.) display before the king the Austrian colours captured in their decisive charge at Hohenfriedberg. The original white dragoon uniform has red facings, and the red horse furniture has white lace with two red stripes. Note the picket-stakes tied to the carbine. (Print after Richard Knötel)

nest' wing and the vertical bars upon the wing. Musicians' hats were like those of the rank and file, with no feathered edging. Drummers carried brass, infantry-style side drums, the carriage being a wide leather belt over the right shoulder, edged with regimental lace, which also ran across the loops which retained the drumsticks; the drums were carried on horseback. Musicians generally used a curved sabre with single-bar guard instead of the *Pallasch*.

Facing colours of the original white uniform were: 1st, black; 2nd, light blue (white lapels); 3rd, red cuffs and lapels; 4th, cornflower blue; 5th and 8th, red; 6th, light blue; 7th, red (white lapels); 9th, light blue (collar and cuffs); 10th and 11th, orange (collar and cuffs). The 1st had dark blue waistcoats.

1st Dragoons

Raised 1689. *Chefs*: Aug. 1725 Hans von Platen; April 1741 Carl von Posadowski (Graf von Posadowski from 1745); April 1747 Bernhard von Katte; Nov. 1751 Johann von Alemann; May 1755 Carl von Normann; April 1761 Johann, Freiherr von Zastrow; June 1774 Friedrich, Graf zu Wylich und Lottum.

Actions: 1, 3, 7, 8, 10, 12, 14, 15, 20, 21.

Uniform: black facings, yellow buttons; sulphur yellow waistcoat, straw yellow breeches. *Other ranks*: red hat-rosettes with white centre; cartridge-box bore oval brass plate bearing crowned eagle over trophy of arms. Light blue shabraque with rounded rear corners, bearing yellow crown over yellow-edged white rococo shield bearing black eagle; same device on holster caps; outer border of yellow lace with three light blue and white checked stripes, inner border similar in chain pattern. *Officers*: gold loops with simulated tassel end. *Musicians' lace*: yellow with black crosses.

2nd Dragoons

Raised 1689. *Chefs*: Aug. 1725 Friedrich, Freiherr von Sonsfeld; Aug. 1742 Prince Louis von Württemberg; May 1749 Reimar von Schwerin; Sept. 1754 Christian von Blanckensee; Sept. 1757 Anton von Krockow; Nov. 1778 Friedrich Wilhelm, Prince von Württemberg; Dec. 1781 Johann von Mahlen.

Actions: 3, 7, 8, 10, 12, 15, 18, 20, 21.

Uniform: white facings, yellow buttons. *Other ranks*: red hat-rosettes; cartridge-box bore oval brass plate bearing crowned 'FR'. White shabraque with rounded rear corners, light blue 'FR' in rear corners and on holster caps, white border with three light blue stripes. *Officers*: gold loops with simulated tassel end. *Musicians' lace*: white with broad yellow stripe between two narrow (wide variety); narrow lace, white with four yellow stripes.

3rd Dragoons

Raised 1704. *Chefs*: Feb. 1724 Adolf von der Schulenberg; April 1741 Friedrich, Graf von Rothenburg; Feb. 1752 Carl, Baron von Schönaich; April 1753 Joachim, Graf

Frederick converses with members of the 5th Dragoons, c.1760. The king frequently exhorted his men on the march with expressions such as 'Exact, children, exact', to which the reply would be, 'Exact, Fritz, exact!' The Bayreuth Dragoons illustrated wear the light blue uniform with red facings, with red horse furniture ornamented with white lace with red lines. (After Knötel)

17

Prussian dragoons charge Austrian infantry, using the same tactic as the cuirassiers—a massed, *closely packed charge with sabres upraised. (After Menzel)*

Dragoons escorting Austrian prisoners on the evening of the Battle of Leuthen; Frederick included in his Instructions the provision for second-line cavalry to *reserve detachments for the reception of prisoners from enemy units destroyed by the charge of the first line. (After Menzel)*

Truchsess zu Waldburg; March 1757 Peter von Meinicke; April 1761 Kurt von Flanss; April 1763 Achaz von Alvensleben; Aug. 1777 Otto von Thun.
Actions: 1, 2, 3, 4, 6, 7, 8, 11, 18.
Uniform: see Plate E1.

4th Dragoons

Raised 1704, reconstructed from 3rd Dragoons 1741. *Chefs*: April 1741 Wilhelm von Bissing; Jan. 1742 Friedrich, Freiherr von Kannenburg; Aug. 1742 Carl, Freiherr von Spiegel; Jan. 1743 Casimir von Bonin; Sept. 1752 Henning von Oertzen; Oct. 1756 Carl von Katte; Oct. 1757 Ernst, Freiherr von Czettritz; Sept. 1772 Georg von Wulffen; Sept. 1782 Carl von Knobelsdorff; May 1786 Carl von Götzen.
Actions: 1, 3, 5, 6, 7, 8, 11, 12, 14, 15, 20, 21.
Uniform: straw yellow facings, waistcoat and breeches, white buttons. *Other ranks*: red hat-rosettes with white centre; cartridge-box bore brass eight-pointed star of Order of Black Eagle. Red shabraque with rounded rear corners, edged with white lace with three light blue stripes. *Officers*: silver oblong loops. *Musicians' lace*: two (for narrow lace) or three (wide) lines of white and light blue checks, with light blue edges.

5th Dragoons

Raised 1717. *Chefs*: Aug. 1731 Friedrich, Erbprinz von Bayreuth (Margrave from May 1735); Aug. 1769 Christian, Margrave of Anspach and Bayreuth.
Actions: 1, 2, 3, 5, 6, 10, 12, 21.
Uniform: carmine facings, straw yellow waistcoat, white buttons. *Other ranks*: yellow hat-rosettes; cartridge-box

bore oval brass plate bearing crowned 'FR' on shield, upon trophy of arms; separate brass grenades at bottom corners of box. Carmine shabraque, bordered by two wide within two narrow white laces. *Officers*: silver embroidered loops with simulated tassel end: two below each lapel, one at each skirt-rear only (none on facings). *Musicians*: see Plate E2.

6th Dragoons

Taken from Saxon service 1717, reputedly in exchange for a cabinet of porcelain, hence regimental nickname of 'Porzellan-Regiment'. *Chefs*: Sept. 1734 Friedrich von Möllendorff; May 1747 Ludwig von Schorlemer; Nov. 1760 Carl von Meier; Jan. 1777 Christian, Baron von Posadowski.
Actions: 3, 9, 14, 18, 22.
Uniform: white facings and buttons, lemon yellow waistcoat. *Other ranks*: red hat-rosettes; cartridge-box bore oval brass plate, bearing crown over eagle over 'FR', over foliate decoration. Light blue shabraque, border of white lace with orange stripe near each edge. *Officers*: silver foliate loops, two below each lapel, one at each rear skirt; loops added to pockets and cuffs 1774. *Musicians' lace*: white with two light blue stripes near each edge (wide); narrow, white with one light blue stripe near each edge.

7th Dragoons

Raised 1727 from 6th Dragoons. *Chefs*: Dec. 1737 Christoph von Thümen; Aug. 1741 Ernst von Werdeck; May 1742 Friedrich von Roehl; Dec. 1745 Erdmann von Ruiz;

Celebrations at the termination of the First Silesian War; the trumpeters appear to belong to a dragoon regiment, although their trumpet banners bearing 'FR' and the elaborate horse furniture are not regulation equipment. (After Menzel)

Aug. 1756 Christoph von Plettenberg; vacant 1761–63; Sept. 1763 Gideon von Apenburg; March 1781 Gottlieb von Borcke.

Actions: 2, 5, 9, 14, 22.

Uniform: red collar, cuffs and turnbacks; no lapels, but yellow buttons arranged as for lapelled coat; straw yellow waistcoat. *Other ranks*: red hat-rosettes. Pink shabraque, border of white lace with orange stripe, orange and white vandycking on each side, white outermost. *Officers*: gold loops with simulated tassel end, including two pairs over four on each side of breast. *Musicians' lace*: red with orange stripe.

8th Dragoons

Raised 1744 from 7th Dragoons. *Chefs*: Nov. 1744 Friedrich von Stosch; Dec. 1751 Adolf von Langermann; March 1757 Dubislav von Platen.

Actions: 5, 9, 14, 18, 21, 22.

Uniform: red facings, white buttons, straw yellow waistcoat. *Other ranks*: red hat-rosettes with white centre. Red shabraque, white lace border with light blue stripe near each edge. *Officers*: silver foliate loops. *Musicians' lace*: white with red wide outer stripes and narrow inner stripes.

9th Dragoons

Raised 1741 from five squadrons of 1st Dragoons, under same commander. *Chefs*: April 1741 Hans von Platen; Oct. 1743 Prince Georg of Holstein-Gottorp; April 1761 Nicolaus von Pomeiske; Aug. 1785 Johann von Zitzewitz.

Actions: 5, 9, 13, 17, 20.

Uniform: see Plate E3.

10th Dragoons

Raised 1743 from 9th Dragoons. *Chefs*: Oct. 1743 Johann von Möllendorff (regiment known as Jung-Möllendorff); Sept. 1754 Friedrich, Graf Finck von Finckenstein; Sept. 1785 Wilhelm von Rosenbruch.

Actions: 5, 9, 13, 17, 20.

Uniform: see Plate E4.

11th Dragoons

Raised 1740. *Chefs*: Dec. 1740 Christoph von Nassau (Graf von Nassau from 1746); Nov. 1755 Christoph von Stechow; March 1758 Leopold von Platen (regiment known as Jung-Platen); Sept. 1770 Franz von Mizlaff; March 1778 Friedrich von Bosse.

Actions: 3, 7, 8, 12, 18, 19, 21, 22.

Uniform: lemon yellow facings, white buttons, straw yellow waistcoat. *Other ranks*: yellow hat-rosettes. Lemon yellow shabraque with rounded rear corners, wide within narrow borders of white lace. *Officers*: silver foliate loops. *Musicians' lace*: yellow with white edges and white vandyck in centre.

12th Dragoons

Taken from Württemberg service 1742; known as 'Alt-Württemberg' until 1749. *Chefs*: June 1749 Friedrich Eugen, Herzog von Württemberg; July 1769 Carl von Reitzenstein; June 1780 Johann von Kalckreuth.

Actions: 4, 7, 8, 10, 12, 19, 21.

Uniform: black plush collar, lapels and cuffs, white buttons, straw yellow turnbacks. *Other ranks*: yellow hat-rosettes. Red shabraque with rounded rear corners, white

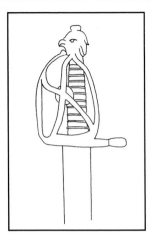

1735-pattern dragoon sabre; brass hilt with eagle-head pommel, and wire-bound leather grip.

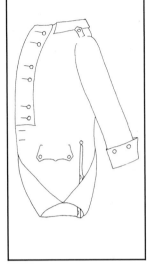

Dragoon coat of the ordinary pattern, of the standard cut used by those regiments which wore lapels. The right shoulder bore an aiguillette at the rear.

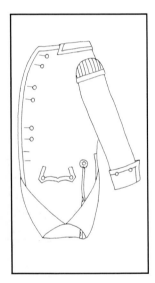

Musician's coat, 9th and 10th Dragoons, two of the three regiments which wore no lapels; the 7th Dragoons' coat was similar, save for the addition of turnback-lace. Note the lace rosette upon which the upper button of the side-vent was set.

lace border. *Officers*: silver foliate loops. *Musicians' lace*: white with edging of yellow (inner) and red (outer) stripes; on the white, black stylized leaf bearing yellow-edged red parallelogram, alternating with red triangles on each side of inner stripe.

HUSSARS

Whereas Frederick inherited most of his heavy cavalry, the lighter regiments were largely his own creation. Hussars in Prussian service originated in 1721, but at Frederick's accession the army included only nine squadrons, three of *Leib-Husaren* and six of *Preussische Husaren*. The value of this type of cavalry was not fully appreciated, so that only six squadrons were fielded at the start of the First Silesian War; finding that these were hopelessly too few to combat the Austrian light troops, and realising that good hussars did not have to be Poles or Hungarians, in 1741 Frederick established five regiments, four from the existing squadrons and the 4th Hussars largely from Polish deserters. Three more were raised by 1744 and another in 1758.

As soon as practicable, all regiments were increased to ten squadrons; from the end of 1743 squadron establishment included 3 officers (4 in each of the six senior squadrons), 8 NCOs, 102 troopers, a trumpeter, a blacksmith and a medical assistant. The regiments were thus very strong, with over 1,100 of all ranks; but they were not always deployed in regimental strength, as even single squadrons could act independently.

The 'Red' regiment was captured at Maxen and disbanded after the peace, the succeeding regiment being re-numbered and the 9th place taken by the *Bosniaken* (see below); a 10th Regt. was formed in 1773. (In the following, the 'Red' regiment is numbered 8th, though it should be noted that some sources number it as the 7th, with the 'Yellow' regiment occupying the number 8, and renumbered as the 7th after the disbanding of the 'Red'. At the time, regimental titles were used in preference to the numbers.)

Although each regiment's uniform was distinctive, the general pattern was similar for all, and based upon traditional Hungarian costume. The headdress was a fur busby for the 1st–4th Regts., and a felt mirliton or *Flügelmütze* for the remainder (also worn by the 4th, 1752–71). Initially the busby was very low, only about six inches deep, but latterly increased to 11 in. for the 1st and 4th and 12 in. for the 2nd and 3rd. The fur was generally medium-brown, usually bearskin, but wolf- and marten-fur were also used. Cords encircled the inside of the top of the cap and fell at the right side, in the button colour (metallic for officers, black and white for NCOs), ending in tasselled raquettes which may have been in squadron colouring, though it is not possible to be precise; all-white cords were certainly worn, if only for the colonel's squadron. A bag in the regimental colour fell at the side or rear.

The mirliton cap was made of black felt, 9–10 in. high for the 6th and 7th and 10–11 in. for the others; the mirliton increased somewhat in size as the period progressed. It had a black triangular 'wing' which was wound around the cap or allowed to fall free, with a button-coloured tassel on the end (black and white for NCOs). Cords, coloured as for the busby, encircled the top of the cap; the wing was edged in metallic lace of the button colour for officers, and black lace for NCOs, who also had a coloured rosette on the front, sometimes worn by officers as well.

Officers on occasion might wear tricorn hats. Plumes, exactly as for the heavy cavalry, were adopted from 1762. Hussars' hair was gathered into a queue, but much shorter than that of the heavy regiments, and the rank and file were permitted to wear twists of hair hanging from the temples; moustaches were worn by all, though musicians are sometimes shown clean-shaven.

The jacket was a tailless dolman (*kamisol*) with a standing collar; there were three rows of buttons on the breast, the central row of 'ball' type and the outer rows flat (occasionally five rows are depicted). Cord frogging or braid edged the collar and pointed cuffs (with or without a loop at the point), and horizontal lines of braid linked the buttons on the breast, these braid loops sometimes interlaced at the ends. Initially the breast-loops were short, but later spread to the extent of the chest.

The number of lines of braid is shown and described differently in various sources and for various years, but varied from 10 to 18. It has been stated that the 1st, 5th and 7th–9th had 12 rows, the 2nd and 3rd 18, and the 4th and 5th 15; or that the 1st, 5th and 7th had 12 rows, the 2nd, 3rd and 8th 14, and the 4th and 6th 15; but no definite distinctions are confirmed by contemporary portraits. Von Kleist, for example (1st, 1759–67), is shown with at least 14 rows, von Wartenburg (3rd, 1745–57) nine or ten, and portraits of the 8th and 9th show 18. As in a number of aspects of hussar uniform, it is likely that many variations existed throughout the period. Officers' lace was metallic, and the extent of decoration was greater than that of the other ranks, generally with 'figuring' around the cuffs in addition to a broad lace cuff-edging, though exact designs of braid seem to have varied widely even within the same regiment. Other ranks had diamond- or heart-shaped leather patches reinforcing the elbows.

Austrian cuirassiers in the uniform worn throughout the period of Austro-Prussian conflict. The similarity of the Austrian cuirassier uniform (like the Prussian, white with coloured facings) caused confusion on the battlefield, resulting in Frederick's concern over the use of 'field signs' and passwords, and latterly the introduction of plumes to distinguish Prussian troops. (Print after R. von Ottenfeld)

The pelisse was worn slung upon the left shoulder in full dress, or could be worn as a jacket; rarely if ever were the dolman and pelisse worn together on active service. The pelisse was braided in a similar fashion to the dolman, and lined and edged with fur. Frederick noted an additional use of the garment: to identify units from the enemy at night, he recommended wearing the pelisse inside-out, or 'putting a piece of white linen on one arm, a green bough in the cap, or choosing some particular word'.

All ranks wore light buff-coloured buckskin breeches in summer and similarly-coloured cloth breeches in winter, with cloth leggings extending to the upper thigh over the breeches. These garments, styled *Sharawaden*, *Charawaden* or *Schalavary*, were edged with lace as on the dolman along the top, and generally until the 1760s often had a heart-shaped patch of the dolman colour, edged with regimental braid, sewn above the knee; latterly a strip of braid was added to the rear seam. These garments are not always depicted, breeches being shown in some illustrations before 1787, when trousers, generally of the pelisse-colour, were introduced; it is likely that the *Sharawaden* were omitted when the pelisse was not worn, for example in summer. The boots were of Hungarian

Hans Joachim von Zieten, 'king' of the Prussian hussars, in the parade uniform of his 2nd Regt., including the unique leopardskin cloak (here *bearing the Order of the Black Eagle) and the eagle-wing and sceptre headdress ornament. (After Menzel)*

The cartridge-box was brown leather (5th black), with a belt of the same, worn over the right shoulder (left by officers and NCOs); when worn, officers' pouches and belts were laced. Troopers carried a plain carbine belt in buff or whitened leather over the left shoulder, with brass fittings and iron carbine-clip. The carbine was generally shorter than that carried by cuirassiers, though the 2nd and 3rd carried weapons of cuirassier length; before the Second Silesian War ten members of each squadron were equipped with rifled carbines. The sabre had a curved blade and iron stirrup hilt, and a wooden scabbard covered with black leather with iron throat and chape. The sword knot was black or brown leather, silver and black for officers. All ranks carried two pistols in holsters beneath the front of the shabraque.

The shabraque had pointed rear corners and no holster caps, in regimental colouring with vandycked edging, in metallic lace for officers. Full dress shabraques for officers were similar, but with a decoration in the rear corners of a gold-crowned white shield bearing a black eagle, but towards the end of the period different patterns of dress shabraques were used by officers. At the rear of the saddle was a cylindrical valise of the shabraque-colour, the circular ends trimmed with regimental braid, resting upon an unbleached fabric fodder-sack. On top of the valise was a folded cloak, which was voluminous and had a wide collar; it was white for all but the 1st, 5th and 6th (dolman-colour). (Frederick disliked white cloaks: 'The cloaks also which the men wear at night, should not be of a bright colour, as the white or yellow shoulder belts render them sufficiently distinguishable.') Harness, in 'Hungarian' style, was black or dark brown leather.

Trumpeters' uniforms were like those of the troopers, with regimental distinctions: 'swallows' nest' wings ornamented with regimental musicians' lace, generally only on the pelisse, and all wore the mirliton, even in regiments which otherwise wore the busby. It is likely that regimental colonels exercised considerably more influence over musicians' uniforms, resulting in variations like the facing-coloured *Sharawaden* and mirliton-wing shown by Menzel for the 5th Regiment. Plumes were originally in regimental colouring, but latterly were either red, or red with white tip (Thieme shows red for the 2nd and 8th). Many conflicting details of trumpeters' uniforms exist, and in the following reference is made to Thieme's illustrations of 1792, which although later than the reign of Frederick are one of several guides to regimental distinctions at the end of the period.

pattern, extending to the bottom of the knee at the front and lower at the back, with iron heels and iron spurs plugged in. In the earlier period officers could wear longer, yellow leather boots in full dress.

The barrelled sash was worn over the dolman but beneath the pelisse, when that garment was worn as a jacket; officers' sashes were silver and black. The waistbelt was made of brown leather, with five slings, to support the sabre and sabretache; officers' belts were covered with metallic lace. The sabretache was generally brown leather (plain black for the 5th and 8th) with a regimentally coloured cloth flap bearing a crowned 'FR' and wide lace edging in the button colour. Officers' sabretaches were more ornate, usually featuring a white shield bearing a black eagle, with a crown above and trophy of arms below, in elaborate metallic embroidery, though economy measures produced officers' sabretaches with similar designs but with less ornate embroidery.

Frederick's carriage with hussar escort, 1740; the hussar uniform at this period includes the original, low busby and heart-shaped decorations upon the Sharawaden. The officer commanding the escort is shown wearing his pelisse over his dolman; it was unusual for both garments to be worn together on campaign. (After Knötel)

In addition to the usual practice of identifying regiments by the name of the colonel, hussar regiments were also known by their uniform-colour, for example *Rote Husaren*.

1st Hussars (Preussisches Husaren, or 'Green Hussars')

Raised 1721 (two coys., attached to 6th Dragoons); three sqdns. 1730, six 1739, eight 1740, ten 1742. *Chefs*: July 1740 Johann von Bronikowsky; Sept. 1747 Otto von Dewitz; Oct. 1750 Michael von Szekely; May 1759 Friedrich von Kleist; 1767–70 vacant; Sept. 1770 Georg, Freiherr von Czettritz.

Actions: 2, 3, 6, 8, 11, 12, 18, 21, 22.

Uniform: originally white with blue facings, and from 1732–42 a uniform like that of the 2nd. Thereafter, busby with dark green bag; 'canary green' (light, yellowish green) dolman and *Sharawaden*, white buttons and lace, dark green pelisse with white fur, crimson sash with white barrels, canary green sabretache laced white; dark green shabraque with canary green vandycks edged white. *Officers*: silver lace, including undulating 'frame' around braiding on breast of dolman and pelisse. *Trumpeters*: see Plate H2.

2nd Hussars (Leib-Husaren or 'Red Hussars', but should not be confused with 8th 'Red Hussars')

Raised 1730 (one coy.); three sqdns. 1733, ten 1742. *Chefs*: July 1741 Hans Joachim von Zieten; March 1786 Carl, Freiherr von Eben und Brunnen.

Actions: 1, 3, 7, 8, 10, 12, 14, 15, 16, 18, 20, 21.

Uniform: busby with red bag. Red dolman; dark blue collar, cuffs, *Sharawaden*; white buttons, braid and lace frame around breast-braid on dolman and pelisse. Dark blue pelisse with white fur (NCOs, brown fox fur); dark blue sash with white barrels; red sabretache with white lace; dark blue shabraque with red vandycks edged white. NCOs: silver lace edging to collar and cuffs, silver braid. *Officers*: gold lace, breast-loops with tassel ends; embroidered dress sabretache as described above, but for ordinary use a red sabretache like that of the other ranks, but with gold lace and cypher; ordinary shabraque like that of other ranks but with gold edging to vandycks, for dress as described before, with gold-crowned white shield bearing black eagle in rear corners. Parade dress: see Plate F3. Officers' harness in red leather with gilt fittings and ornamented with cowrie shells (worn by all ranks).

Prussian hussars engage Austrian skirmishers, 1745; the Prussians at this period wear the low busby, and for active service have discarded both the pelisse and Sharawaden. (After Menzel)

Trumpeters: mirliton with silver lace edging and red or mixed red and white plume; dolman with white or red and white mixed braid, and collar- and cuff-lace and breast 'frame' in silver with two red stripes; same lace on pelisse on cuffs, breast-frame, wings, and inverted chevrons on the sleeves. Thieme shows white lace with two red stripes, with silver outer edges. Trumpet-cords mixed silver and red.

3rd Hussars

Raised 1740 (1 sqdn. from 1st Hussars); 10 sqdns. 1742. *Chefs*: July 1740 Friedrich von Bandemer; Sept. 1741 Hyacinth von Malachowski; April 1745 Hartwig von Wartenberg; Sept. 1757 Carl von Warnery; March 1758 Christian von Möhring; May 1773 Stephan von Somoggy; Dec. 1777 Hans von Rosenbusch; Sept. 1785 Carl von Keöszegy.

Actions: 7, 8, 12, 20, 21.

Uniform: busby with white bag; white dolman and pelisse-fur; yellow collar, cuffs, buttons and braid; dark blue *Sharawaden*; dark blue sash with white barrels. Yellow sabretache with white lace; dark blue shabraque with white vandycks edged yellow. *NCOs*: gold lace on collar and cuffs, and undulating gold 'frame' around breast-braid on dolman and pelisse; some sources indicate pelisses trimmed with red fox-fur, but regulations note white for all. *Officers*: see Plate G1. *Trumpeters*: mirliton with gold-edged wing, mixed yellow and blue plume; Thieme shows a red and yellow rosette and white plume with red tip. Braid mixed red and yellow; yellow lace with two red stripes on cuffs and frame of dolman and pelisse, on dolman collar, and on wings and five chevrons on pelisse sleeves. (Some sources note that bright green facings and

Sharawaden were worn until c.1757, though a portrait of von Wartenberg which includes the earlier, low busby shows the yellow facings in use even then).

4th Hussars ('White Hussars')

Raised 1741 as lancers ('*Corps Hulaners*'), six sqdns.; converted to hussars 1742. *Chefs*: July 1741 Georg von Natzmer; Feb. 1751 Heinrich von Vippach; Sept. 1755 Georg von Puttkamer (killed in circumstances of great gallantry at Kunersdorf); Dec. 1759 August von Dingelstädt; Nov. 1762 Balthasar von Bohlen; Sept. 1770 Carl von Podjurski; March 1781 Prince Friedrich Eugen of Württemberg.

Actions: 3, 4, 7, 8, 12, 15, 16, 18.

Uniform: mirliton 1752–71, otherwise busby with light blue bag, which some sources indicate was worn before its official sanction in 1771. Light blue dolman and *Sharawaden* (some sources indicate white *Sharawaden* until later 1750s), white pelisse with white fur (black until late 1750s), braid mixed light blue and white; light blue breeches with mixed white and light blue braid shown 1758. Crimson sash with white barrels, white sabretache laced light blue, white shabraque with light blue vandyck edged with mixed light blue and white braid. *NCOs*: silver cuff lace, light blue rosette on front of mirliton. *Officers*: silver lace, including double undulating 'frame' on dolman and pelisse; light blue mirliton rosette, black pelisse-fur; light blue sabretache (presumably for ordinary use) with light blue vandycks edged silver, bearing gold crowned white shield bearing gold-crowned black eagle. *Trumpeters*: silver-laced mirliton with mixed white and light blue plume, mixed light blue and white braid; white lace with light blue edges on pelisse-wings, and some sources indicate sleeve-chevrons, not shown by Thieme (but by this date, 1792, light blue pelisses were in use, introduced 1787); Thieme shows light blue and red mirliton rosette. Trumpet cords light blue and white (light blue sashes with white barrels shown before late 1750s).

5th Hussars ('Black' or 'Death Hussars')

Raised 1741 from sqdns. of 1st and 2nd Hussars. *Chefs*: March 1744 Joseph von Ruesch (Freiherr from 1753); May 1762 Friedrich von Lossow; Oct. 1783 Carl von Hohenstock.

Actions: 3, 9, 13, 14, 16, 17.

Uniform: mirliton bearing white skull over crossed bones on front. Black dolman, pelisse, sharawaden, pelisse-fur and leatherwork, red collar and cuffs from 1772, white

1 Officer, 8th Cuirassiers
2 Officer, 11th Cuirassiers, Galarock
3 Officer, 13th Cuirassiers (Garde du Corps), Galarock, post-1762

A

1 Standard-bearer, 13th Cuirassiers (Garde du Corps), post-1762
2 Officer, 13th Cuirassiers (Garde du Corps), post-1762
3 Trumpeter, 10th Cuirassiers (Gens d'armes)
4 Officer, 12th Cuirassiers, post 1762

B

1 Trooper, 5th Dragoons, 1745
2 Trooper, 7th Cuirassiers
3 Trooper, 2nd Cuirassiers

1 Trooper, 6th Dragoons
2 Officer, 4th Dragoons, 1750
3 Officer, 1st Dragoons

D

1 Trooper, 3rd Dragoons, post-1762
2 Drummer, 5th Dragoons
3 Trooper, 9th Dragoons
4 NCO, 10th Dragoons

1 Trooper, 5th ('Black' or 'Death') Hussars, 1744
2 Trooper, 2nd Hussars
3 Field Officer, 2nd Hussars, Gala Dress

F

1 Officer, 3rd Hussars
2 Trooper, 'Red' Hussars
3 Trooper, 'Total Death' Hussars
4 Trooper, 7th Hussars

G

1 Officer, 6th Hussars, post-1762
2 Trumpeter, 1st Hussars
3 Trooper, Bosniaks, summer uniform, post-1762
4 Officer, Bosniaks, winter uniform, post-1762

H

buttons and braid, red sash with white barrels; plain black sabretache; black shabraque with red vandycks edged white. *NCOs*: silver cuff-lace, white rosette on mirliton instead of skull. *Officers*: silver lace, including mirliton rosette and double undulating 'frame' around breast-braid on dolman and pelisse; sabretache for ordinary wear black with silver crowned 'FR', red vandycked border edged silver. *Trumpeters*: white plume and mirliton wing-edging, mixed black and white braid, white lace with two black stripes on wings and dolman cuffs (red stripes later, presumably after adoption of red facings); pelisse with white fur lining but black edging. 1752 Regulations note white lace, silver mirliton-lace, white and black feather; Thieme shows a trumpeter with no wings, red and white braid, red lace 'frame' and red mirliton with black wing lined red, red-tipped white plume, and red/white/black rosette. A post-Seven Years' War source shows red mirliton cords with yellow tassels (squadron identification?), and officers with fur busby with red bag, and white pelisse-fur.

6th Hussars ('Brown Hussars')

Raised 1741. *Chefs*: March 1742 Isidor, Graf von Hoditz; Aug. 1743 Carl von Soldan; Aug. 1746 Ludwig, Freiherr von Wechmar; Feb. 1757 Johann von Werner; Jan. 1785 Johann von Gröling.

Actions: 3, 5, 7, 8, 12, 15, 21.

Uniform: mirliton; brown dolman, *Sharawaden* and pel-isse; yellow collar, cuffs, braid and buttons; white pelisse-fur; yellow sash with white barrels. Brown sabretache with yellow lace, brown shabraque with yellow vandycks. *NCOs*: gold cuff-lace, yellow rosette on front of mirliton. Officers: see Plate H1. Trumpeters: mirliton with gold wing-lace, blue and yellow plume, yellow and white braid; white lace with two yellow stripes on wings. Yellow and white trumpet cords. (The shade of uniform colour was originally a pale, greyish brown; dark brown was not introduced until 1803.)

7th Hussars ('Yellow Hussars')

Sometimes listed as the 8th, and replacing the disbanded 'Red Hussars' as the 7th. Raised 1743. *Chefs*: April 1744 Peter von Dieury; April 1746 Heinrich von Billerbeck; Aug. 1756 Paul von Malachowski; Dec. 1775 Adolf von Usedom.

Actions: 5, 7, 9, 12, 14, 16, 17, 18. (This provides an example of how a regiment could serve in two campaigns simultaneously, by the fact that squadrons could act independently of each other: two squadrons only served with the Allied army at Minden as part of a composite hussar unit.)

Uniform: mirliton; lemon yellow dolman, lightish blue pelisse and *Sharawaden*, white braid and buttons, light blue collar and cuffs after 1771. Light blue sash with white barrels; light blue sabretache laced white; light blue shabraque with yellow vandycks edged white. *NCOs*:

Prussian hussars in combat during the early campaigns; note the low busbies and omission of pelisses and Sharawaden. The officer, falling wounded in the foreground, has a plume and busby-decoration of the type shown in the portrait of Wartenberg as Chef of the 3rd Hussars, referred to in the text. (After Menzel)

silver cuff-lace, light blue mirliton rosette. *Officers*: silver lace, including double undulating 'frame' around breast-braid on dolman and pelisse, light blue mirliton rosette; light blue dress sabretache bearing silver crown over black eagle upon silver trophy of arms, within silver foliage, scalloped silver lace border. Officers' shabraque light blue with silver lace edging. *Trumpeters*: silver edge on mirliton wing, light blue and yellow plume; braid mixed white and light blue, white lace with two light blue stripes on wings.

8th Hussars ('Red Hussars')

Raised 1743. *Chefs*: Nov. 1743 Sigismund von Hallasz; Sept. 1747 Alexander von Seydlitz; April 1759 Otto von Gersdorff. Disbanded after Seven Years' War.

Actions: 3, 8, 10, 11, 12, 19. (This is an example of a unit serving in several major actions but not at regimental strength: two sqdns. at Rossbach, three at Breslau, five at Kolin and Leuthen.)

Uniform: mirliton; darkish red dolman, pelisse and *Sharawaden*, white braid and buttons, black pelisse-fur; red sash with white barrels; plain black leather sabretache; red shabraque with red vandycks edged white. Cartridge-box belt worn over left shoulder, the same as the carbine belt. *NCOs*: silver cuff-lace, red mirliton-rosette. *Officers*: silver lace, including double undulating 'frame' around breast-braid; sabretache (presumably for ordinary use) red, bearing crowned 'FR' and border in silver. *Trumpeters*: silver lace edging to mirliton wing, mixed white and red plume; mixed white and red braid, white lace with two red stripes on wings.

9th Hussars ('New Black' or 'Whole Death' Regt.)

Raised 1758; re-numbered 8th after disbandment of 'Red' Regt. *Chefs*: Jan. 1761 Wilhelm von Belling (who had commanded from the beginning); Dec. 1779 Carl von Hohenstock; Oct. 1783 August von der Schulenberg.

Actions: Kunersdorf (5 sqdns.), Freiberg (10 sqdns.).

Uniform: see Plate G3. Mirliton with white device on front, or a reclining skeleton and motto 'Vincere aut Mori'; as this badge was more extensive than the skull of the original Death Hussars (5th), the unit was known as *der ganze Tod* ('the whole Death')! Black dolman, pelisse, *Sharawaden* and sash, yellow buttons, light green braid, white pelisse-fur. Black leather sabretache bearing light green crowned 'FR' and border; black shabraque with light green vandycks. *NCOs*: light green rosette on mirliton instead of skeleton; gold lace edging to cuffs shown by Menzel. *Officers*: gold lace, black pelisse-fur, light green collar and cuffs; black sabretache for ordinary use bearing gold crowned 'FR', light green vandycked border edged gold. Officers' shabraque for full dress, black with green vandycks edged gold, bearing gold-crowned white shield emblazoned with gold-crowned black eagle in rear corners; ordinary shabraque similar, with gold crowned 'FR' instead of shield. *Trumpeters*: braid mixed black and

Members of the 1st Hussars loot the French baggage at Gotha, 15 September 1757; note the pelisses worn as jackets, and the low size of the busby at this period. (After Knötel)

Prussian hussars (foreground) perform one of their principal tasks: pursuing an enemy in retreat and preventing him from rallying. (After Menzel)

yellow, yellow lace with two black stripes on wings and cuffs. From 1764 the regiment adopted the uniform of the previous 'Red' Regt.

10th Hussars

Raised 1773. *Chef*: Aug. 1773 Carl von Owstien.
Uniform: busby with yellow bag; yellow dolman; dark blue collar, cuffs, pelisse and *Sharawaden*; white buttons and pelisse-fur; red braid, including 'frame' around breast of dolman and pelisse; crimson sash with dark blue barrels; dark blue sabretache bearing red crowned 'FR', yellow vandycked border edged red; dark blue shabraque with yellow vandycked border edged red. *NCOs*: silver cuff-lace. *Officers*: silver lace; ordinary shabraque as other ranks but silver vandycks. *Trumpeters*: mirliton with red plume, mixed red and blue braid, red lace with oblique blue stripes on 'frames' and on pelisse-wings. Thieme shows a silver-laced mirliton with red rosette and red-tipped white plume, a fringed 'frame' on the dolman, and no wings.

BOSNIAKEN

Ranked as 9th Hussars from 1771. One of the most unusual units in the army, the Bosniaks were raised for Saxon service by an Albanian jeweller named Stephan Serkis, who recruited some lancers in the Ukraine. Unable to enlist in Saxon service, he offered his men to Frederick, who attached a squadron of them to the 5th Hussars in 1745. The corps was enlarged to ten squadrons by 1763, but their performance was not outstanding and they reverted to squadron strength. Increased to five squadrons in 1770, the unit was allocated the number 9 in the list of hussar regiments and increased to ten squadrons in 1773, but remained associated with the 5th Hussars until granted

its own *Chef* in 1788; prior to that date, its colonel was that of the 5th Hussars.
Uniform: The original Bosniak uniform was a semi-oriental style, which was retained even when Germans and various deserters were recruited; many variations are depicted in various sources. Originally, it included a white turban around a red skull-cap, with a mixed red and white feather at the left; a dolman-length red jacket with white lace edging around the collar and cuffs and down the breast and bottom edge, the pointed cuffs bearing a white loop, and the breast without buttons; and Turkish-style, baggy red trousers with white lace on the outer seam. Over the jacket was worn a long-skirted black overcoat with folding collar and wide, elbow-length sleeves, with white lace around the edges and on the bottom of the sleeve. Equipment was black leather, including a cartridge-box which bore a white 'FR' cypher; black shabraque with red vandycks, and similar holster caps, which in addition bore a white 'FR'. Three tassel-ended laces were borne on the breast of jacket and overcoat by officers and NCOs, in silver and white lace respectively.

The semi-oriental appearance was retained in the unbraided red jacket and baggy trousers, both laced white as before, the trousers latterly having vertical side-pockets piped white, and white piping around red cloth reinforcing around the ankle. Some sources indicate the use of mirlitons, but latterly a dark brown fur cap was worn (sometimes shown as black); although this was probably not introduced until after the Seven Years' War, perhaps as late as 1780, some sources date it at least as early as 1762. This busby had no hanging bag but a red cloth crown, with white cords and raquettes hanging at the right (Menzel shows light green, presumably squadron colouring), with

plumes as worn by the other cavalry from 1762. Other ranks wore a red girdle (officers a silver and black sash); black leather equipment continued to be used, the cartridge-box belt over the left shoulder (right for NCOs), troopers having a white carbine belt over the left shoulder, to the spring clip of which was attached a pistol. Officers wore a very long, red frock coat with three rows of buttons and silver hussar-braid on the breast, and silver piping outlining the vertical side-pockets, with black cuffs and falling collar piped silver.

This red uniform was summer dress; in winter, all ranks wore a very long, black frock coat with black cuffs. The falling collar and lining were off-white or pale grey fur, with white piping down the breast (no buttons), around the bottom edge and on the vertical pockets. NCOs had silver lace on the upper edge of the cuffs (as on the red summer jacket), and three tassel-ended white lace loops on each side of the upper breast; the girdle was worn over this garment. The officers' winter frock coat was black with silver piping to the cuffs, around the pockets and down the front and bottom edges, with a red folding collar, piped

silver. The breast bore three rows of buttons and tassel-ended loops of hussar-style braid. The winter frock coat is sometimes described as very dark blue, but this colour did not replace the black until 1787, when narrower, white trousers and black sabretaches were also introduced.

Trumpeters were dressed like the troopers, with black wings on the original overcoat, bearing white lace with a red stripe; the red mirliton had a black wing, red rosette on the front and a white plume with red base. Later, the summer uniform was like that of the troopers (including busby with red-tipped white plume), but with mixed red and white piping and with the musicians' lace on collar and cuffs; latterly this was white with two red stripes. The black winter coat had mixed red and white piping, musicians' lace on the cuffs, and three mixed red and white, tassel-ended loops on the upper breast.

Lances were carried by the unit, usually depicted with the shafts painted in red and black spirals, with a variety of swallow-tailed pennons which were apparently coloured according to squadron or company: among recorded designs are black, white, light green, orange, crimson, red, green over red or white, white over red, and black over yellow. Officers' and NCOs' lances had pennons of black over white, the black bearing a golden sun and the white a gold-crowned, flying black eagle. For officers the pennons were made of silk, and the lance-shafts painted white.

STANDARDS

As in the infantry, each regiment carried a number of standards, one per squadron (*Eskadronstandarte*), with one designated the *Leibstandarte* or colonel's standard. Standards were not renewed automatically upon the accession of a new monarch, so that some bearing the 'FWR' cypher remained alongside newer examples bearing 'FR'.

Devices were similar for both patterns: an oval silver centre bearing a black eagle with gold crown, flying towards a gold sun on the earlier pattern, and with outspread wings, holding a sword and with a gold crowned 'FR' on its breast for the newer pattern; above the eagle was a scroll of the ground-colour of the standard, bearing 'Non Soli Cedit' on the older, and 'Pro Gloria et Patria' on the newer pattern. The oval centre was surrounded by a metallic wreath (green and metallic for cuirassiers) with a metallic crown with red cap above; a crowned cypher within a metallic wreath (green for cuirassiers), sometimes on a silver ground, was placed in each corner. For some regiments, straight-edged or undulating 'rays' formed a saltire from the corners.

Leibstandarte were white, with the central panel of the *Eskadronstandarte* ground-colour, with the same devices. Standards were square for cuirassiers and swallow-tailed for dragoons, both with metallic fringe. The poles were of the standard's ground-colour, topped with fretted gilt spear-heads bearing the cypher as on the standard; two streamers attached below the spear-head were silver and black. (The length of service of Prussian flags was such that 1740-pattern infantry colours remained in use until the very end of the Napoleonic Wars). Colouring was as the accompanying Table A:

Table A: Cuirassier & Dragoon Standards

Regiment	colour	decoration	remarks
1st Cuirassiers	yellow	gold	
2nd Cuirassiers	dark red/purple	silver	yellow straight rays
3rd Cuirassiers	white	gold	
4th Cuirassiers	dark red/purple	gold	
5th Cuirassiers	light blue	gold	white straight rays
6th Cuirassiers	dark blue	gold	
7th Cuirassiers	red	gold	
8th Cuirassiers	black	gold	gold eagle on centre of *Leibstandarte*
9th Cuirassiers	sea-green	gold	
10th Cuirassiers	gold	gold	
11th Cuirassiers	dark blue	gold	
12th Cuirassiers	orange	gold	
13th Cuirassiers	Vexillium: see Plate B1		
1st Dragoons	yellow	gold	
2nd Dragoons	yellow	gold	red straight rays
3rd Dragoons	white (Menzel, rose-pink)	gold	*Leibstandarte* with rose-pink centre
4th Dragoons	white	gold	*Leibstandarte* with blue centre
5th Dragoons	black	gold	
6th Dragoons	light blue	gold	gold undulating rays
7th Dragoons	black	gold	red undulating rays
8th Dragoons	black	gold	red undulating rays
9th Dragoons	yellow	silver	red undulating rays
10th Dragoons	orange	silver	red straight rays
11th Dragoons	yellow	silver	silver undulating rays
12th Dragoons	red	silver	

*Cuirassier standard, 'old'
pattern, with eagle and sun
centre, 'Non Soli Cedit'
motto and 'FWR' cyphers;*

*as carried in the Seven
Years' War by the 1st, 3rd,
4th, 8th, 10th, 11th and 12th
Regiments.*

*Cuirassier standard, 'new'
pattern, with 'Pro Gloria et
Patria' motto and 'FR'
cyphers; with the straight-*

*edged 'rays' of the
Eskadronstandarte of the
2nd and 5th Regiments.*

(The earlier patterns were carried during the Seven Years'
War by the 1st, 3rd, 4th, 8th, 10th, 11th and 12th
Cuirassiers, and 1st, 2nd, 3rd, 4th and 7th Dragoons.)

Until 1743 hussar regiments carried swallow-tailed
guidons, all with a contrastingly coloured, vandycked

edge. Central devices were the same as for dragoons, with
motto-scroll in the ground colour, and crowned cypher
within a wreath in each corner; *Leibstandarte* were white
with the centre of the ground colour of the *Eskandronstan-
darte*. See Table B for details.

*Dragoon standard, 'old'
pattern, with the straight-
edged rays of the
Eskadronstandarte of the
2nd Regiment.*

Table B: Hussar Guidons

Regiment	colour	vandycked edge	decoration
1st Hussars	dark green	light green	silver
2nd Hussars	blue	red	gold
3rd Hussars	blue	yellow	gold
4th Hussars	light blue	white	silver
5th Hussars	black	red	silver
6th Hussars	brown	yellow	gold

THE PLATES

A1: Officer, 8th Cuirassiers

A regiment made famous by its colonel, Seydlitz, the 8th had dark blue facings and silver lace. This shows two regimental distinctions: red cuirass-edging instead of in the facing colour (though Menzel shows blue), and turnbacks with dark blue lace for officers, instead of in the button colour. Typical horse furniture is depicted (after Knötel), with a silver-laced shabraque; the officer does not carry the valise and cloak at the rear of the saddle, as did the other ranks.

A2: Officer, 11th Cuirassiers, Galarock

This illustrates a typical *Galarock* as worn by cuirassier officers, always in true white instead of the off-white or straw yellow of the *Kollet*. In the earlier period the *Galarock* is often shown worn completely open, exposing the whole of the waistcoat; later it appears with the lapels closer together, or even closed at the upper breast. This officer carries the *Pallasch* with the *Galarock*, though lighter swords could be used with this order of dress.

A3: Officer, 13th Cuirassiers (Garde du Corps), Galarock, post-1762

Only the officers of the 10th and 13th Cuirassiers wore a scarlet *Galarock*, that of the Garde du Corps being by far the most magnificent. It had dark blue facings (but no lapels); foliate-embroidered silver loops with simulated tassel end, eight on each lapel and two on the cuff, pocket flap and rear waist; a silver aiguillette; and dark blue lining, visible when the tails were turned back, a somewhat later practice. The hat has the 1762 plume, and the lace and

Dragoon standard, 'new' pattern, with the undulating 'rays' of the 4th, 8th, 9th, and 11th Regiments.

Frederick instructs a hussar regiment in review; for a 'dress' occasion the pelisses are worn slung over the left shoulder. The busbies shown are now larger than the original type, but still lack the plumes adopted from 1762. (After Menzel)

white feather edging worn with the *Galarock*; the officer carries a lighter sword in place of the *Pallasch*.

B1: Standard-bearer, 13th Cuirassiers (Garde du Corps), post-1762

Standards were normally carried by NCOs or junior officers; this *Standartenjunker* has the double silver cuff lace, black and white sword knot tassel and black-tipped plume of NCO rank, but wears the cartridge-box belt over the same shoulder as the troopers, not in NCO fashion, in order to accommodate the standard belt; these were of metallic lace of the button colour with facing-coloured stripe, and metallic fringe. The Garde du Corps standard was in the form of a *vexillum*, suspended from a horizontal bar from a pole topped by a sculpted, silver eagle.

B2: Officer, 13th Cuirassiers (Garde du Corps), post-1762

As a mark of their 'household' status, for ceremonial palace duty the Garde du Corps wore the ordinary *Kollet* without the cuirass, with a sleeveless *supreveste* or tabard over the top. For all ranks it was red with silver lace decoration down the front, side seams, on the bottom edge and around the neck- and arm-holes, with a large, silver-embroidered star of the Order of the Black Eagle on the breast (with orange centre bearing a black eagle, green wreath below and 'Suum Cuique' above). For officers the lacing was

especially fine; the garment had a silver fringe around the bottom edge, and was worn with a laced hat with feathered edge. For dismounted guard duty the other ranks wore black knee-gaiters and carried muskets. The unit's sabres were of cuirassier pattern but with white metal hilts.

B3: Trumpeter, 10th Cuirassiers (Gens d'armes)

This illustrates a typical trumpeter's uniform, like that of the other ranks but minus the cuirass (thus revealing the lace edging to the breast), plus the hanging sleeves and musicians' lace; for the 10th, hat-feathers were red and the lace gold with one or two red stripes for narrow and wide varieties respectively. Trumpeters' swords are often depicted as being lighter than the ordinary *Pallasch*.

B4: Officer, 12th Cuirassiers, post 1762

This depicts a typical cuirassier officer's uniform, with the plume adopted in 1762 and the regimental orange facings and gold lace. The cuirass is sometimes depicted, especially in the later period, worn under the *Galarock* instead of with the *Kollet*.

C1: Trooper, 5th Dragoons, 1745

The original white dragoon uniform is illustrated here, worn by a trooper of the famous Bayreuth Dragoons, perhaps the most effective of Frederick's cavalry. They won immortal fame at Hohenfriedberg, when for the loss of less than a hundred men their charge overturned part of the Austrian army, capturing five fieldpieces, 2,500 men and 67 Colours. Frederick described them as 'Caesars'; but part of their effectiveness lay in the fact that the unit was twice the ordinary establishment of a dragoon regiment. Having almost brigade strength they had not been included in the more restrictive order of battle, but were permitted to act as a cavalry reserve, and thus were able to execute their charge independently.

C2: Trooper, 7th Cuirassiers

This shows the ordinary cuirassier uniform, with the buff-leather carbine belt ornamented with the same regimental lace as borne upon the *Kollet*. Except for the polished cuirasses of the 13th, cuirasses were enamelled black with facing-coloured edging (except for the 8th), either enamelled or in the form of fabric 'cuffs'; ruched fabric edging was worn only by officers.

C3: Trooper, 2nd Cuirassiers

Alone of the cuirassier regiments, the 2nd wore coats of a strong yellow shade, hence the nickname *Gelbe Reiter*. Evidence exists for this unit of the company identification by the troopers' sword knot tassels, though in general such identifications are not clear. The fringe was white, with the 'bell' above identifying the squadron (red, blue, black, yellow or green), companies within the squadron having either a coloured 'bell' or one with a white central portion. Illustrated here is the position of the shoulder strap, generally set to the rear of the shoulder on the *Kollet*.

D1: Trooper, 6th Dragoons

This member of the famous 'Porcelain Regiment' wears the light blue uniform worn throughout most of Frederick's reign, and depicts the typical horse furniture of heavy regiments, with blackened harness. Although the design of shabraque varied, in other respects the equipment was standard, including the carbine carried with its muzzle in a small bucket below the right holster, with a

Upright plumes appear to have been worn as indications of senior commissioned rank even before the general introduction of plumes from 1762, as in this engraving after Menzel, showing the mirliton with wing unwound.

strap around the butt securing it to the saddle. An iron-shod picket stake was strapped to the carbine.

D2: Officer, 4th Dragoons, 1750

Shown here is the earlier style of dragoon uniform, soon after the adoption of the light blue coat, with lapels having a curved bottom edge. The hat is the original tricorn, without the later flattening of the front corner, and is shown by Menzel with a silver lace edging. The boots of the earlier period sometimes appear slightly higher and narrower than later, a style which even extended to hussar officers, who are depicted with boots of hussar cut but above knee length.

Although Frederick put great emphasis for even outlying parties of cavalry to remain in formed bodies, elements of hussar squadrons could skirmish in open order, firing carbines from the saddle. (After Menzel)

Charge of the 'Black' or 'Death' Hussars (5th Regt.) at Gross-Jägersdorf. Although the details of uniform are observed accurately, many non-contemporary illustrations depict the use in combat of both dolman and pelisse, whereas it would appear that they were rarely used together on campaign.

D3: Officer, 1st Dragoons

A slightly later style than that shown in Plate D2, this includes the coat with skirts turned back. Menzel's depiction of this uniform includes the 1762 plume and coat-loops of semi-undulating foliate design; but a portrait of the regimental *Chef* Johann von Alemann (1751–55) clearly shows the tassel-ended loops, and in addition a gold-laced hat with white feathered edge, and gauntlets of a shade even darker than the sulphur yellow of the waistcoat.

E1: Trooper, 3rd Dragoons, post-1762

The 3rd Dragoons (shown here with the 1762 plume) wore pink facings and hat-rosettes and white buttons; the cartridge-box bore a brass, eight-pointed star of the Order of the Black Eagle. Shabraques were pink with rounded rear corners, with a wide inner and narrower outer border of white lace. Officers wore silver foliate loops. Musicians' lace was white with pink diamonds, and a pink stripe near each edge.

E2: Drummer, 5th Dragoons

When mounted, the infantry-style side drums of dragoon drummers were suspended from the drum belt at the left side. Musicians' lace was worn only on the facings and wings, with the rear skirt buttons set upon lace rosettes; for the 5th, musicians' lace was silver with two red stripes. Drum hoops were not invariably striped white and the facing colour, as here: the 2nd, for example, are shown with white hoops bearing a blue zigzag line with red 'tripods' within the Vs of the zigzag; the 4th with alternate light blue and white diagonals; and the 9th the same but with two red stripes on the white diagonals.

E3: Trooper, 9th Dragoons

The 9th was one of three regiments not to wear lapels, but the only one to have no contrasting facing colour and lace button loops for all ranks, which are shown by Menzel as very wide, with rounded ends. Two pairs of four loops were carried on the breast, and two on the cuff, pocket flap and rear waist; hat-rosettes were light blue with white centre, and waistcoats straw yellow. The light blue shabraque had pointed rear corners, and a border of white lace with a red stripe near the edges. NCOs' coats were laced as for other ranks, but in silver. Officers wore silver foliate loops with simulated tassel ends. Musicians' lace was white with light blue edges and an undulating stripe; they wore no button-loops.

E4: NCO, 10th Dragoons

This NCO wears the usual rank distinctions: black and white hat-rosettes and sword knot tassel, metallic lace on the cuff, and no carbine belt. Regimental distinctions for the 10th were: orange collar, cuffs and turnbacks, no lapels; white buttons; yellow waistcoat. Other ranks had orange hat-rosettes with light blue centre. The orange shabraque had a white lace border. Officers wore silver foliate loops with simulated tassel ends, two pairs over four on breast, two on cuff and rear waist. Musicians' lace was white with an orange stripe and light blue edges.

F1: Trooper, 5th ('Black' or 'Death') Hussars, 1744

This figure, after Knötel, shows an early uniform, when the mirliton is often depicted somewhat lower and narrower at the top than it became later. This shows a typical summer campaign uniform, with pelisse and *Sharawaden* omitted; alternatively, the pelisse could be worn as a jacket in place of the dolman. The death's-head badge on the mirliton gave rise to the regimental sobriquet, 'Death Hussars'. The regiment's *Leib*-Company rode white or grey horses, despite Frederick's advice that for nocturnal operations 'no dogs or white horses should be allowed', or anything to indicate their position to the enemy.

F2: Trooper, 2nd Hussars

The 2nd Hussars were famous for having the great hussar Zieten as their *Chef* for almost 45 years. Alone of the hussar regiments, save the 10th raised in 1773, the 2nd was distinguished by the use by all ranks of the 'frame' of lace worn around the braid of both the dolman and pelisse.

F3: Field Officer, 2nd Hussars, Gala Dress

For parade dress officers of the 2nd wore yellow boots (a quite common colour in the earlier period), and instead of the pelisse a cloak made of an entire leopard-skin lined with crimson fabric and edged with sable, worn over the left shoulder and fastened under the right arm. Upon the skin gilt stars, heart, sun and crescent moon were affixed. Squadron commanders and regimental staff officers wore a singular ornament in the busby: an eagle wing upon a gilt staff resembling a sceptre, tipped with a crown over a pierced 'FR' cypher, the eagle feathers supported by a gilt framework at the base of the sceptre; it continued to be

Trooper, 1st Hussars: apparently a facsimile copy of an illustration by C. C. Horvath, 1789, showing the hussar uniform at the end of the Frederickian period, with the plume introduced from 1762. The 'canary green' dolman and darker green pelisse have white braid; the sabretache bears the 'FWR' cypher of Frederick's successor.

worn in full dress instead of the plume adopted in 1762. Menzel shows the sceptre affixed to the busby internally, but an extant cap has a gilt tube fixed to the outside.

G1: Officer, 3rd Hussars

Officers of the 3rd wore gold lace, including an undulating 'frame' around the breast-braid on pelisse and dolman. In addition to the elaborately embroidered yellow sabretache (shown by Menzel with a blue ground) officers had a plainer version: yellow with a gold-crowned white shield bearing a black eagle, with plain gold lace border. A portrait of Hartwig von Wartenberg (*Chef* 1745–57) illustrates the earliest style of headdress, a squat brown busby with white bag and short white plume (presumably indicative of rank) rising from a large, jewelled ornament at the left front of the cap. The braid on the dolman breast is narrow, the buttons at this date being set closer together horizontally than later, and the pelisse has no lines of braid but merely the 'frame' and loops hanging from the buttons. He wears a gold-covered pouch-belt over the left shoulder, which Menzel's version of the portrait shows as white with gold edges.

G2: Trooper, 'Red' Hussars

Sometimes numbered as the 7th, the 'Red' (numbered

here as the 8th) was disbanded following its surrender at Maxen, the previous 'Whole Death' regiment filling its place and adopting its uniform. Recorded variations on the uniform include an officer's portrait lacking the 'frame' of lace on the breast but with five rows of buttons, and silver-laced pouch- and sword-belts with red edging. Shown here are the lace hearts sometimes worn on the *Sharawaden*, which were often present in the earlier years; and note the regimental practice of wearing the cartridge-box- and carbine-belts over the same shoulder.

G3: Trooper, 'Total Death' Hussars

The 9th gained their nickname from the reclining skeleton on their mirlitons, in effect going one stage further than the original Death Hussars (5th) whose badge was a death's-head. The shape of this device is shown differently; Menzel depicts the skeleton reclining with the head to the right, upon the motto 'Vincere aut Mori', while another version

Trooper, 7th Hussars. This study is typical of the uniform illustrations of Adolph Menzel, executed more than 60 years after the end of the reign of Frederick the Great. Although accurate, in many cases they depict uniforms of the later part of the period, in this case, *for example, showing the light blue facings added to the 7th's yellow dolman from 1771. At the right are NCO rank distinctions: silver cuff-lace, silver and black sword knot, and mirliton bearing a blue rosette on the front and a white plume with black tip.*

A story used to illustrate the stalwart conduct of the Prussian army concerned the capture by the French of a wounded 'Black' Hussar in 1758. He was interrogated about Prussian strength by the French Prince Clermont, who asked, 'How strong is your king?' 'As strong as steel and iron.' 'How many are your comrades?' 'As many as the stars in the sky.' Clermont asked in admiration, 'My friend, does your king possess other soldiers as brave as you?' The hussar replied that he was only a poor example, or else he wouldn't have been taken prisoner. (After Knötel)

Frederick greets Zieten at Torgau, after the latter had been given semi-independent command of a large proportion of Frederick's army, and had virtually saved Frederick from defeat. Zieten (right) wears the uniform of his 2nd Hussars, with the pelisse as a jacket for winter service, and a white cloak; and carries the dress version of the officers' sabretache, bearing a black eagle on a white shield, backed by a gold-embroidered trophy of arms and with scalloped gold lace edging. (Print after Carl Röchling)

shows it with scythe and hourglass. Menzel also shows green facings, worn only by officers, black pelisse-fur, and yellow barrels and cords on the sash. The mirliton at this period (c.1758) is slightly smaller and narrower at the top than the size it attained later.

G4: Trooper, 7th Hussars

This 'Yellow Hussar' depicts the reverse of the hussar costume in general; note the leather reinforcing usually carried on the elbows and rear cuff of the dolman. This unit was one of the hussar regiments with white cloaks (the 1st had green, the 5th and 'Total Death' black, the 6th brown), despite Frederick's aversion to this colour, believing them too visible, especially at night.

H1: Officer, 6th Hussars, post-1762

This officer of the 'Brown' Hussars wears the 1762 plume, and the mirliton rosette worn in the facing- or braid-colour by NCOs (dark blue for the 7th), and by officers in metallic or coloured lace; an alternative for the 6th is shown as black. The fringed 'frame' around the breast is shown in contemporary sources, but others indicate double undulating lace. Their dress shabraque was like that of the men with, in the rear corners, a gold-crowned white shield bearing a gold-crowned black eagle, upon a gold-embroidered trophy of arms. In addition to the embroidered sabretache, another version included the same device as on the shabraque, upon a brown ground, with yellow vandycked edge.

H2: Trumpeter, 1st Hussars

Details of trumpeters' uniforms are complicated, and much conflicting evidence is present, presumably indicating changes of decoration during the period. For the 1st Regt. braid was mixed white and green, with white lace with two green stripes on the wings. All trumpeters wore mirlitons, here with green and white plume and white wing-edging; Thieme shows a green rosette with red edge and centre.

H3: Trooper, Bosniaks, summer uniform, post-1762

In essence, this uniform (after Menzel) is very similar to that worn originally, but for the replacement of the turban by a busby, and the absence of the black frock coat with elbow-length sleeves and white lace edging, originally worn over the red jacket. The uniform still retained an exotic element, most notably in the Turkish-style, voluminous trousers. The fur cap may have been introduced as late as 1780, but some sources indicate its use as early as 1762; white cords are sometimes depicted, but Menzel shows light green, perhaps a company colouring reflected in the lance-pennon, one of many recorded variations.

H4: Officer, Bosniaks, winter uniform, post-1762

The black frock coat worn in winter shown here has the red folding collar of officers, in place of the white fur collars of the other ranks; Menzel shows an alternative with black

An Austrian hussar in campaign uniform: the similarity with Prussian hussar uniform was another cause of confusion on the battlefield, which Frederick made serious attempts to prevent. (After Von Ottenfeld)

standing collar edged all round with silver lace, and with additional braid on the breast. Officers wore similar coats in scarlet, with black collars and cuffs, in summer; and although Menzel shows the universal waist sash, other sources indicate a silver girdle without hanging tails.

SOURCES

Invaluable works, essential for any study of Frederick the Great and his army, are the two modern volumes by Christopher Duffy: *The Army of Frederick the Great* (Newton Abbot, 1974) and *Frederick the Great: A Military Life* (London 1985); the same author's *Military Experience in the Age of Reason* (London 1987) forms an excellent background to the period. The work of the leading modern German authority, Hans Bleckwenn, is equally invaluable; for uniforms, the illustrations of *Das Altpreussische Heer*, available as *Die friderizianischen Uniformen* (Osnabruck 1987) are incomparably the finest work available. Frederick's army has attracted the attention of some of the great illustrators, most notably Adolph Menzel, whose plates, executed in the middle of the 19th century, were published with a text by C. Jany in *Die Armee Friedrichs des Grossen in iher Uniformerung* (Berlin 1908). The other great illustrator, Richard Knötel, featured Frederickian uniforms in his plates, and also in *Der Alte Fritz in 50 Bildern für Jung und Alt* (Berlin 1895), a work of the highest calibre of book-illustration, executed in collaboration with Carl Röchling.

Useful biographies of Frederick include *Frederick the*

Great (Nancy Mitford, London 1970), and Thomas Carlyle's *History of Friedrich II of Prussia, called Frederick the Great* (London, 1858–65) is still of value. *The Pictorial History of Germany during the Reign of Frederick the Great* (F. Kugler, London 1845) includes anecdotal material and illustrations by Menzel. Frederick's writings can probably be found most conveniently in *Military Instructions from the late King of Prussia to his Generals* (trans. T. Foster, London 1797) and *Particular Instruction of the King of Prussia to the Officers of his Army, and especially those of Cavalry*, both reprinted in a combined edition, London 1818. *Die Kavallerie-Regimenter Friedrich des Grossen 1756–1763* (G. Dorn & J. Engelmann, Friedberg 1984) includes useful regimental histories. The booklet *Prussian Cavalry, Seven Years War: Dragoons and Curassiers* (sic) (R.D. Pengel & G.R. Hurt, Birmingham 1981) is a useful

Frederick's last interview with the old Zieten. Zieten and his aides wear the uniform of his 2nd Hussars, the general with the yellow boots of full dress; and all three hussars illustrate the practice of wearing a tricorn hat in some orders of dress, instead of the busby. On one occasion the old hussar, who died only a short time before Frederick himself, fell asleep at the king's table; Frederick remarked, 'Let him sleep; he watched long enough over us.' Upon the death of the old hussar, and reflecting upon his own approaching end, Frederick said, 'Our old Zieten has shown himself a good general even in death. In the wars he always commanded the advance guard; he has taken the lead now, too . . .' (After Röchling)

guide, drawn to a considerable extent from Bleckwenn. An interesting assessment of Frederick's use of cavalry is *The Cavalry of Frederick the Great: Its Training, Leading and Employment in War*, W.H. Greenly, in Cavalry Journal Vol. VI (London 1911).

Farbtafeln

A1 Zu den Besonderheiten des Regiments gehören rote Küraß-Einfassungen (anstatt in Bortenfarbe); dunkelblaue Spitzen auf den Stulpen (anstatt in Knopffarbe). Siehe typische Ausstattung für Offizierspferde. **A2** Der Galarock war stets reinweiß; im Lauf der zeit wurde er so getragen, daß die Rockaufschläge eng beisammen oder sogar geschlossen waren. **A3** Nur dieses und das 10. Regiment trugen den scharlachroten Galarock; der hier abgebildete ist wesentlich dekorativer als der des 10.Regiments. Man beachte den mit dieser Kleidung getragenen Hut.

B1 Ausrüstung für Unteroffiziere – siehe Manschetten, Schwertquaste und Feder – aber er trägt Patronentaschengürtel wie die Kavalleristen (nicht Unteroffiziere), um den zusätzlichen Fahnengürtel aufnehmen zu können, in Knopffarbe und Besatzfarben. **B2** Die Supreveste ersetzt den Küraß – ein Zeichen der Leibwache-Zugehörigkeit – und trägt den Schwarzen Adlerorden. Beim nicht-berittenen Dienst trugen die Kavalleristen schwarze Gamaschen und waren mit Musketen bewaffnet. Diese Uniform wurde nur für zeremoniellen Palastdienst getragen. **B3** Typische Trompeter-Uniform: kein Küraß, hängende Ärmel, andere Spitzen und Hutfedern. **B4** Nach 1762 wurde der Küraß manchmal unter dem Galarock getragen.

C1 Bayreuther Dragoner in der weißen Originaluniform; diese doppelt-starke Einheit erwarb sich bei Hohenfriedberg hohen Ruhm. **C2** Diese geschwärzten Kürasse hatten Einfassungen in Farbe der Aufschläge, entweder emailliert oder als Stoffstreifen. Karabinergürtel waren mit derselben Spitze wie das Kollet verziert. **C3** der feste gelbe Mantel war typisch für diese Einheit; siehe hintere Position des Schulterriemens. Die Schwadronsfarben an der Schwertquaste waren entweder rot, blau, schwarz, gelb oder grün.

D1 Typische Pferde- und Sattelausstattung für schwere reiterei. **D2** Der frühe Stil der hellblauen Dragoneruniform zeigt Aufschläge mit gekurvtem unteren Rand; originaler Dreispitz ohne die spätere Abflachung der vorderen Spitze; etwas höhere und engere Stiefel wie später. **D3** Späterer Uniformstil; dies beruht auf einem Portrait des Regiments-Chefs, das den Menzel-Abbildungen in einigen Einzelheiten widerspricht.

E1 Siehe Regimentsabzeichen in weiß und rosa. **E2** Zu Pferd trugen diese Dragoner-Trommler zur Linken Infanteriertrommeln; die Trommelriemen waren nicht unbedingt wie hier weiß gestreift. Musikanten-Spitzen nur an Rändern udn Aufschlägen des Mantels, und den rückwärtigen Knöpfen. **E3** Eines der drei Regimenter ohne Aufschläge, und das einzige ohne ohne kontrastierende Besatzfarben, aber mit Spitzen- Knopflochschlingen für alle Ränge. **E4** Übliche Unteroffiziers-Rangabzeichen am Hut, Schwertquaste und Manschette; kein Karabinegürtel. Die 10. Dragoner hatten Rangabzeichen in Orange, keine Aufschläge und gelbe Weste.

F1 Frühe Uniform nach Knötel, mit niedrigerem schmäleren Mirliton als später. Dies ist eine Sommer-Felduniform, ohne Pelisse oder Sharawaden. **F2** Zietens Regiment zeigte einen 'Rahmen' von Spitzen rund um die Borten von Dolman und Pelisse. **F3** Die erstaunliche Paradeuniform dieses Regiments, mit gelben Stiefeln, Leopardenfellumhang und – für Schwadronskommandeure und andere Offiziere – einer Adlerschwinge auf dem Kolpak.

G1 Nach einem Vergleich zwischen Gemälden von Menzel, und einem Portrait von Hartwig von Wartemberg, Chef der Einheit von 1745–57; folgt man hauptsächlich für das frühe Aussehen der Uniform. **G2** Portraits variieren in Details; siehe hier die Spitzen-Herzen am Sharawaden, in früheren Jahren oft zu sehen; und die Gewohnheit dieses Regiments, Karabiner- und Patronentaschengürtel über dieselbe Schulter zu werfen. **G3** Die Einzelheiten des Skelett-Abzeichens am Kolpak waren unterschiedlich, wenn man den Quellen Glauben schenken darf. Menzel zeigt Offiziere mit grünen Aufschlägen, schwarzem Pelissenpelz und gelben Schnüren an der Schärpe. **G4** Typische Rückenansicht einer Husarenuniform; siehe Lederverstärkungen.

H1 Manche Quellen zeigen Spitzen in doppelten Wellenlinien als Brustumrahmung, wie als Fransen. **H2** Es gibt viele widersprüchliche Quellen für die komplexen Trompeteruniformen. **H3** Nach Menzel; die Pelzmütze ersetzte ab etwa 1762 den Turban, und der schwarze, weißbesetzte kurzärmelige Mantel, früher über der roten Jacke getragen, wurde abgeschafft. **H4** Der rote Mantelkragen wurde von Offizieren getragen – andere Ränge hatten weiße Pelzkragen. Im Sommer konnten Offiziere ähnliche Mäntel tragen, aber in Scharlachrot mit schwarzem Kragen und Manschetten.

Notes sur les planches en couleur

A1 Les particularités régimentaires comprennent un liseré rouge (à la place de la couleur du parement) sur la cuirasse; et un passement bleu foncé (au lieu de la couleur du bouton) sur les retroussis; notez l'harnachement du cheval caractéristique d'un officier. **A2** Le Galarock a toujours été en blanc net; avec le temps on commença à le porter les deux revers fermés ensemble, ou même boutonnés. **A3** Seuls ce régiment et le 10ème portaient le Galarock écarlate, celui de l'illustration étant bien plus décoratif que celui du 10ème. Notez les détails du chapeau porté avec cette tenue.

B1 Distinctions de sous-officiers – voir les manchettes, la dragonne et la plume – mais la ceinture de la cartouchière est portée de la même façon que le font les hommes de troupe (qui ne sont pas des sous-officiers) pour recevoir la ceinture supplémentaire standard. Ceux-ci étaient de la même couleur que les boutons et les parements. **B2** La supreveste remplaçant la cuirasse, signe de rang de la Garde, porte l'ordre de l'Aigle Noir. Pour les missions à pied, les hommes de troupe portaient des guêtres noires et des mousquets. Cet uniforme se portait seulement pour les services officiels au palais. **B3** Uniforme caractéristique de trompette; pas de cuirasse, manches tombantes, passement différent et plumes de chapeau. **B4** Après 1762, la cuirasse se portait parfois sous le Galarock.

C1 Dragon de Bayreuth dans un uniforme blanc d'origine; cette unité double s'est couverte de gloire à Hohenfriedberg. **C2** Les cuirasses noircies avaient un liseré de même couleur que le parement, soit émaillé dessus, ou en bandes de tissus; seuls les officiers portaient des fronces. Les ceintures des mousquetons étaient ornées de passement comme sur le Kollet du régiment. **C3** Le vif manteau jaune était particulier à cette unité; et notez la position arrière de la patte d'épaule. Les couleurs de l'escadron sur le gland de la dragonne étaient rouge, bleu, noir, jaune et vert en séquence.

D1 Harnachement de cheval caractéristique de la cavalerie lourde et équipement de selle. **D2** Le premier style d'uniforme des dragons bleu clair avec des revers ayant un bord arrondi en bas; chapeau tricorne d'origine, sans l'effet aplati du coin avant qui fut ajouté plus tard; bottes légèrement plus hautes et plus serrées que celles qui suivirent. **D3** Style plus tardif d'uniforme; celui-ci est basé sur un portrait du Chef de régiment, qui contredit Menzel dans quelques détails.

E1 Notez les distinctions roses et blanches de ce régiment. **E2** Les tambours des dragons portaient, à cheval, le tambour de l'infanterie du côté gauche; les cercles de tambour n'étaient pas toujours à rayures blanches et de la couleur du parement. Passement des musiciens sur les parements et les pans du manteau seulement, et comme renfort pour les boutons de dos. **E3** L'un des trois régiments sans revers, et le seul sans couleur de parement contrastant, mais avec des boucles de boutonnières en passement pour tous les grades. **E4** Distinctions de grade courante des sous-officiers sur le chapeau, la dragonne et les manchettes; pas de ceinture de mousqueton. Les distinctions d'unité du 10ème étaient orange, sans revers et avec un gilet jaune.

F1 Premier style d'uniforme, d'après Knotel, avec un mirliton plus bas et plus étroit que celui représenté par la suite. C'est une tenue de campagne pour l'été, sans pelisse ou sharawadens. **F2** Le régiment de Zeiten avait un 'contour' de passement autour des brandebourgs du dolman et de la pelisse. **F3** L'étonnante grande tenue de parade de ce régiment, avec bottes jaunes, manteau en peau de léopard, et pour les commandants d'escadron et les officiers d'état-major une aile d'aigle sur la coiffure.

G1 D'après une comparaison de tableaux par Menzel, et un portraitiste inconnu de Hartwig von Wartenberg, Chef de l'unité de 1745 à 1757, et suivant principalement ce dernier pour le tout premier aspect de l'uniforme. **G2** Les portraits varient en ce qui concerne les détails; notez ici des coeurs en passement sur le sharawaden, que l'on vit souvent dans les premières années; et notez comment cette unité avait coutume de porter en bandoulière sur la même épaule les ceintures à mousqueton et à cartouchière. **G3** Les détails de l'insigne de chapeau à squelette variaient, si l'on peut en croire les sources. Menzel montre les officiers avec des parements verts, une pelisse noire en fourrure et une ceinture à olives jaunes. **G4** Vue de dos caractéristique d'une tenue de hussard; notez les renforts de cuir.

H1 Certaines sources présentent des lignes doubles ondulantes de passement encadrant la poitrine, as de frange. **H2** Il y a de nombreuses sources contradictoires pour les détails des uniformes complexes des trompettes. **H3** D'après Menzel; le chapeau de fourrure a remplacé le turban à partir de 1762 environ, et le manteau noir, à garniture blanche et à manche courte qui se portait auparavant sur la veste rouge a été abandonné. **H4** Le col de mantgeau rouge distinguait les officiers – les hommes de troupe portaient des cols de fourrure blanche. Les officiers portaient en été des manteaux similaires à celui-ci mais de couleur écarlate avec col et manchettes noirs.